Assessing Writing, Assessing Learning

A Practical Guide for Evaluating and Reporting on Writing Instruction Programs

Dudley W. Reynolds
Carnegie Mellon University Qatar

Ann Arbor
The University of Michigan Press

Published in the United States of America
The University of Michigan Press
Manufactured in the United States of America

♾ Printed on acid-free paper

ISBN-13: 978-0-472-03420-8

2013 2012 2011 2010 4 3 2 1

Contents

Tables and Figures

TABLES

FIGURES

Introduction

In schools and universities around the world, writing is taught as a stand-alone subject. It is also used to test everything from engineering to social work. The centrality of writing for both what and how we learn in academic settings demands that we develop effective practices for assessing it. Many of us have good systems in place for grading and responding to student papers; we know what is important to comment on and what distinguishes a better paper from a less successful paper in our discipline. We may be less confident, however, when it comes to rendering judgments on what students know about writing as a practice. Too often we view the course grade as a necessary evil. When asked to "prove" that students have learned something about writing, we complain about cost-benefit analyses of education instead of seeing the request as an opportunity for reflection. We may also turn to commercial tests as an easy solution without due consideration of what they measure and how that matches with what we should want to know.

This book addresses *how to assess writing as a practice.* It presents a systematic process for identifying what we need to know, tools for discovering it, and suggestions for how to take advantage of what we have learned. It is written for audiences who do not consider themselves to be "assessment specialists" and contains numerous worksheets, examples, links to further information, and a glossary of terms. Much of the material was developed when I worked with a newly established writing center at the University of Houston as its Director of Research and Assessment. At the time, the Writing Center was working hard to show the university community the benefits of focused writing instruction at all academic levels and within the applied context of a discipline. Under the leadership of Dr. Marjorie Chadwick, we became entrepreneurs, asking units across campus what they needed and how we could create an instructional program that would fit their unique setting. The result was a wealth of experience in design and implementation and lots of lessons in academic politics. I came to that job with a research interest in the development of writing abilities by speakers of English as a second language (ESL) and a professional interest in preparing prospective teachers to work in the myriad contexts where ESL students enter our educational systems. You will see these experiences reflected again and again in this book. Assessing writing as a practice requires thinking of assessment as a cyclical process of design, implementation, reporting, and improving; it also requires that we consider carefully what writing is and how it functions in social contexts.

From beginning to end, *Assessing Writing, Assessing Learning* is a product of collaboration. Where others have authored a specific example or tool, I have acknowledged it. But collaboration is not just about generating products; it is also about opening doors, shaping visions, and providing moral (and financial) support. This book would not have been written without the opportunities provided by the University of Houston Writing Center and my colleagues there: Marjorie Chadwick, Steve Liparulo, Robert Askew, Jennifer Wilson, Kyung-Hee Bae, Mary Gray, Colley Hodges, Michele Miley, Bobbie Chun, Kelly Bracy, and Long Bao Nguyen. Debts of gratitude also go to Libby Barlow, John Antel, Tamara Fish, and j. Kastely at the University of Houston. This book would not have been completed without the opportunities to engage in collaborative and reflective practice provided by Carnegie Mellon University Qatar. For this I must thank everyone from the Dean's Office to my fellow faculty and my colleagues in the English Department at our Pittsburgh campus. I also gratefully acknowledge the support of the Qatar Foundation for Education, Science and Community Development. Their financial support has been essential, but their encouragement to think, innovate, and create has been inspiring.

Why This Book

There are two primary ways this book may be used: (1) as a professional development resource for teachers, administrators, and writing support staff who need to know how to assess a program of writing instruction, and (2) as a practical tool for those actively engaged in developing an assessment plan for a writing program. As such the book combines a theoretical overview of assessment as process and practice with hands-on resources that can be used without modification. The three main chapters—Planning, Tools, and Reporting—suggest a heuristic for identifying and sequencing tasks. At the same time, the figures, worksheets, and links to further information provide the material for going beyond thinking about assessment. Suggestions for how the book might be used in different contexts follow.

Professional Development

Ideally, planning for assessment should be an integral part of planning any program of instruction. How we will measure learning is as important as which textbook we will use and the sequence of topics. As a resource for teacher training programs and professional development workshops, this book is therefore highly appropriate. It outlines a three-step process of planning, designing/implementing, and then reporting on assessment. It also builds a practical knowledge of the abilities and techniques involved in each of these phases.

Pre-Service Pedagogy Course

Many academic departments provide graduate students with a course on the pedagogy of the discipline. In fields where it is common to use writing assignments to measure learning, this book may be used to supplement discussions of developing course objectives, differences between formative and summative assessment, the importance of reliable assessment practices, and the politics of education. In fields where writing is assigned but rarely taught, this book can also be useful for helping students to think about what they should respond to when they grade an assignment. Because many of the students in these pedagogy courses may not have a lot of experience in course design or teaching, it may be helpful to adopt a case-based approach. Ask students to work though the process leading to an assessment plan for a scenario like the ones listed on pages 1–3. Give students a different scenario, and ask them to choose and develop an appropriate instrument for assessing a particular type of data; then ask them to use the instrument they've developed with work produced by students in the discipline and to write up a report about what they discovered. The links to further information could also be assigned as topics for brief reports.

In-Service Training

In-service teachers are more likely to have had some training in educational measurement and, depending on the discipline, theories of effective writing practices. They may have trouble, however, seeing the forest for the trees. They may be very good at explaining why a piece of writing is more or less effective, but less certain about what a student knows about writing. Additionally, while in-service teachers may be good at explaining why they do an individual activity, they may not regularly link those explanations to an overall theory of learning or have a systematic way of showing to others that students have gained what they assume the students are gaining. This book provides guidance in both of these areas. The planning worksheets associated with Chapter 2 can be used to challenge teachers to frame their activities and assessment methods in terms of student learning. Teachers might also be asked to try a tool from Chapter 3 that they do not regularly use and then report back to the group on what they learned. Finally, using some of the resources in Chapter 4 on Reporting, they might be asked to role play different scenarios where they have to justify to a particular audience what they are doing in their classes.

Practical Tool

Pre-service and in-service training in assessment provides teachers with a place to start, a heuristic for questions they should be asking. Often, however, we find ourselves trying to find a way to assess a program that needs to start next week or one that has been going on for several years but no one ever asked us to report on its effectiveness. At this point we are no longer developing a theory; we are trying to write an instrument or identify something that we are already doing that could provide evidence of effectiveness. Whether we are a program coordinator in a writing center, part of a departmental assessment committee, or a course teacher, this book is designed to be something we can pull off the shelf to quickly double-check a definition, to peruse for inspiration, or to find a particular example to modify. The chapter and section titles are transparent and organized according to where we are in the sequence of planning, implementing, and reporting.

CHAPTER 1

An Introduction to Understanding Assessment

Why Do You Need This Book?

Do any of the settings, characters, or concerns in these scenarios sound familiar to you?

- The Assistant Director of a Writing Center has been asked by the Dean of the College of Architecture to set up a program that will help senior architecture majors with proposal writing. The faculty is not happy with the proposals students are writing for the major's capstone course but can't see how they could fit writing instruction into the course. The Writing Center sees this as an opportunity to offer more than walk-in tutoring services and so would like to be able to tout the program's successes to other colleges.
- A graduate student in Rhetoric and Composition at a U.S. university has been asked by the chair of her department if she would be interested in helping set up a college preview program for high school juniors at a new campus the university has established in Azerbaijan. The goals of the program are to recruit students to the university and introduce them to the practices and assumptions of U.S. style education. Students in the program would work on the kinds of essays needed for college applications and standardized admission tests. The chair tells her that it would be a great résumé builder.

- A high school English teacher runs a grant-funded summer program each year for students who fail the writing component of the state-mandated exit exam. Many of the students speak English as a second (or third) language and are new to the U.S. education system. The program allows for more individualized attention and the extra practice that the students need. The teacher and his principal feel that the program is working, and a number of the students are passing the exam the second time around. The grant agency acknowledges the program's success but has warned the teacher and principal that it may not be able to continue funding. The teacher and the principal want to provide the agency with additional evidence of the program's successes.
- At a new English-medium university in an African country with a rapidly expanding economy, the Director of First-Year Writing has been asked by the President's office to report on the program's effectiveness to the university's funders. The funders want to monitor what students are learning in the program. The Director wants to identify areas where the program is successful but would also like to make a pitch for funding to create a Writing Center and to improve the existing curriculum.
- The Biology Department's Director of Undergraduate Studies is concerned that the graduate teaching assistants who staff lab sections for the general education biology course do not know how to grade or respond to the writing in lab reports. The Director is willing to ask members of the English Department and Writing Center for advice but knows that she will not be able to pay them to run a program without outside funding. She wants to put a teacher training component into a grant proposal she is writing but feels that she needs some preliminary findings that would show promise of success.
- The Director of a university-based, Intensive English Program (IEP) has been asked by the Assistant Provost for Academic Affairs at the university's research hospital if a program could be set up for doctors who are non-native speakers of English to help them with writing medical articles for publication. The hospital has studied the publication acceptance rate of its physicians and found that native-speaker status was a significant predictor of acceptance. The IEP is self-funded and would like to run more community programs.
- The English professor for the writing pedagogy course required of all graduate students teaching in the first-year writing program realizes that many of the students, who are pursuing PhDs in literature and rhetoric, will end up working in or running a composition program. The professor knows that such

> programs are constantly competing for resources and so are asked to provide evidence of student learning. The graduate students have not had much exposure to empirical research, and the professor feels that they need tools to construct evidence-based arguments. As a course project, she requires them to write a report documenting student progress in the first-year classes they are currently teaching.

Effective writing is central to educational and professional success in our globalized society. We must pass the writing component of gatekeeping exams to graduate from high school, enter college, and be admitted to graduate schools. Whether we are studying biology or hotel and restaurant management, we must use a writing process to help us organize our thoughts, and we must produce written reports to demonstrate learning. In business settings, reputations are enhanced by the clarity and concision of writing, and sales are made on the nuances of appeals.

It is no wonder, therefore, that so many people take an interest in how writing is taught. Some of these individuals are writing professionals—Writing Center personnel, Rhetoric and Composition faculty and graduate students, Language Arts teachers, ESL instructors and program administrators. Others don't see themselves on the front line of instruction, but they know good writing when they see it and believe in its importance. They include faculty and administrators for academic units across campus, parents, employers, and state and federal legislators. Finally, students themselves want to know what is expected of them on writing assignments and how they can improve.

It is also no wonder that across academic settings myriad strategies and solutions exist for how to teach writing and systematically improve the learning of writing. These strategies and solutions are referred to in this book as "programs." They may be conceptualized as a series of training workshops for teachers, a credit-bearing class such as first-year composition, required visits to the Writing Center, or an after-school club. Wherever such a program exists or is initiated, there usually also exists a need to make sure the program is accomplishing what was envisioned for it and a desire to see if it can be improved. *Assessing Writing, Assessing Learning* will fill this need.

This book is a guide to assessing and evaluating writing and writing-related instruction in academic settings. Effective assessment does not just test what students already know or have learned how to do; rather, it opens up the whole learning process for inspection. It is the implementation of a principled process that leads to curricular innovation and individual development. It involves considered decisions about inputs and constraints, the systematic collection and interpretation of data, and follow-through on the insights that have been gained. In short, assessing writing should mean assessing learning.

The goals of this book are broader than many standard books on writing assessment, which focus on evaluating an individual's ability to create an effective piece of writing for a particular purpose. (For suggestions on works that deal primarily with evaluating written texts, see the Further Reading section at the end of this chapter.) This book seeks to support teachers, administrators, program directors, and funding entities who want to make the best use of the resources at their disposal to understand what students are learning and why and then take actions based on what they have learned. It also seeks to provide a common basis for communication among all the interested parties—the writing professionals, the people who identified the need for the program, and the students.

Assessing Writing, Assessing Learning was originally written for the staff at the University of Houston Writing Center, and many of the examples contained herein were developed as part of its highly successful Writing in the Disciplines Program. I fully recognize, however, that on different campuses writing programs and writing assessment may fall to English departments, interdisciplinary units, task forces, offices of institutional research, and any number of other groups. As much as possible I have tried not to make assumptions about who the stakeholders for writing assessment may be. I have simply assumed that their common stake is a desire to promote student learning and develop quality programs.

Guiding Principles

Many assessment regimes bear little resemblance to the holistic process outlined in this book. Anyone in this field knows about locally developed **placement tests** put in place about 15 years ago that generate a numerical evaluation that no one can explain in terms of what it means a student can and cannot do. We may dread having to produce an annual **institutional effectiveness** report because we know that the outcomes were chosen simply because they were the easiest to gather data on and fail to capture a majority of what goes on in our program. Or perhaps you are frustrated by the hours you spend grading and writing comments on portfolios at the end of a semester because you know there is a 50 percent chance a portfolio will sit in a box in your office all of next semester never to be claimed by the student. Too often these efforts began with the good intention to improve assessment, but without a clear understanding of why we should be assessing or the essential characteristics of effective assessments.

The suggested practices and examples in this book are designed to support a program where assessment serves learning, and they build from these premises:

- Planning for assessment should be an integral part of designing a program, not an afterthought.
- **Formative** as well as **summative** ends should be considered in an assessment plan.
- The selection and reporting of assessment tools should be based on a detailed understanding of a program's goals, its participants, and the relation between the program and the larger curriculum.
- Assessments are data-based inferences, and having multiple types of data increases their certainty.
- The potential consequences of assessment findings for individuals as well as programs should always be considered when planning, and the actual use of the findings should be monitored after they have been reported.

Organization

These guiding principles are addressed in three sections:

- *Chapter 2: Planning* discusses program-related variables, the formulation of goals, purposes of assessment, and writing up of an assessment plan.
- *Chapter 3: Tools* describes different ways of collecting data for assessment purposes and provides links to example instruments.
- *Chapter 4: Reporting* discusses issues related to making data-based inferences and provides example formats for reporting.

Each of these principal sections is further subdivided into related topics. For each topic, a discussion of issues and advice for working through the issue are provided along with numerous examples. A list of resources to consult for more information about a topic is also provided.

Chapter 5 provides a collection of worksheets that can be reproduced and used to help the people in charge of setting up and delivering a program think through the issues presented here. Finally, there is a glossary at the end for all terms that appear in bold.

Resources

Further Reading

American Educational Research Association. (1999). *Standards for educational and psychological testing.* Washington, DC.

Hamp-Lyons, L. (2002). The scope of writing assessment. *Assessing Writing, 8*(1), 5–16. doi: 10.1016/S1075-2935(02)00029-6.

Shaw, S. D., & Weir, C. J. (2007). *Examining writing: research and practice in assessing second language writing.* Cambridge, UK: Cambridge University Press.

Weigle, S. C. (2002). *Assessing writing.* Cambridge, UK: Cambridge University Press.

White, E. M. (1994). *Teaching and assessing writing: Recent advances in understanding, evaluating, and improving student performance* (2nd ed.). San Francisco: Jossey-Bass.

Wolcott, W., & Legg, S. M. (1998). *An overview of writing assessment: Theory, research, and practice.* Urbana, IL: National Council of Teachers of English.

www.ncte.org/positions/writing—The National Council of Teachers of English is the leading association for writing professionals and has prepared a number of position statements about the teaching and assessment of writing. Its major conference is CCCC (Conference on College Composition and Communication).

www.tesol.org > Issues > Position Statements—Teachers of English to Speakers of Other Languages (TESOL) has also published a number of position statements on the assessment of English language learners.

CHAPTER 2

Planning

> Effective assessment provides useful information for multiple audiences, supports both short-term and long-term development, and makes the most efficient use of resources.

Developing a Plan

This chapter covers the development of an assessment plan for a writing program. Too often a **questionnaire** is administered or students are asked to provide a writing sample without a clear sense of what will be learned and whether that is what we really need to know; in the end we find ourselves asking, "So what?" This is partly why assessment activities should be based on a comprehensive plan involving a detailed analysis of the program's curricular and disciplinary context, a clear articulation of the program's goals, and an understanding of how the findings will be reported and used.

Taking the time to formulate and write a plan provides a document that can be shared and excerpted with all the stakeholders and also provides a head start on any follow-up reporting. This may seem like an overly bureaucratic step, but at the last week of the semester when you may be trying to wrap up three different programs, you will be grateful for a written record of what you promised to do and when you promised to do it by.

The Process for the Plan

The process of plan development has six chronological components:

1. **Program Description**—Start with considering basic issues like how the program is or will be set up and what could reasonably be accomplished given the type of setup.
2. **Goals**—Articulate statements about what participants will gain from the program, which will determine what should be measured.
3. **Formative Activities**—What types of information could be generated during or at the end of the program that would help participants get more out of it?
4. **Summative Activities**—What types of information do the various stakeholders—including the students—expect at the end of the program?
5. **Resource Evaluation**—Once we have thought about possible activities, we need to conduct a reality check. Rating essays, focus groups, running a statistical analysis—all require significant commitments of time, equipment, and sometimes physical space.
6. **Writing the Plan**—Bring everything together into a concise, written document.

Program Description

> Ethnographic methods based in recursive analyses of the artifacts and processes of a particular context are frequently used in educational research to provide deeper insights and generate hypotheses.

Parameters

Program description involves creating a narrative understanding of a program's structure and context that focuses on features with the potential to influence learning. These parameters may be useful components to consider:

- degree of embedding within the curriculum—Does the program draw participants from a particular course, a degree program, an academic unit (e.g., a college-wide program), or the university at large?
- student recruitment—Are students required to attend, or is attendance voluntary? If required, will everyone attend or only selected individuals? How has this been explained to the participants?

- nature of interaction—Does the program primarily involve presentation of material (e.g., a workshop, online resources), is the program more interaction based (e.g., consultations), or does it incorporate both? (The answer to this question may also relate to whether the program is focused on content mastery or the development of writing abilities.)
- intensity—How many opportunities will students have to interact with program content and/or instructors and over what period of time? Is the program designed to provide a general introduction or sustainable changes in behavior?
- perspective on writing in student's context—Do students have frequent opportunities to write outside the program? Is writing thought of as a way to promote and demonstrate learning? How important are discipline-specific conventions or genres? How important is writing to students' future or current employment?

Resources

Chapter 5 Worksheets

The *Program Description Worksheet* (page 102) provides a place to record answers to some of the basic questions suggested. Oftentimes people who do not specialize in the teaching of writing think of writing as a skill that a student either has or does not have. A worksheet like this can be used to help teachers develop a more realistic set of expectations for a writing program.

Further Reading

Atkinson, D., & Ramanathan, V. (1995). Cultures of writing: an ethnographic comparison of L1 and L2 university writing/language programs. *TESOL Quarterly, 29*, 539–568.

Watson-Gegeo, K. A. (1988). Ethnography in ESL: Defining the Essentials. *TESOL Quarterly, 22*(4), 575–592.

http://wpacouncil.org/—The Council of Writing Program Administrators is a professional association for program administrators. Its website has lots of useful information about issues that affect writing programs, the role and mission of writing programs, and the assessment of writing.

Goals

Goals provide measurable outcome statements for student learning.

Parameters

Assessment activities must be based in an understanding of the expectations for a program, and goals articulate expectations in a way that is measurable. As you formulate goals, start by considering where the program directs its attention and how it articulates its reason for being. What does it say is important? These parameters may be helpful:

- focus of program—Does the program seek to improve specific skills/abilities/characteristics, or is the focus more on global development? Related to this, does the program seek to redress past deficiencies in instruction or simply move someone along a developmental continuum?
- orientation toward writing—When you describe the content of the program, do you highlight tasks (e.g., producing abstracts), skills (e.g., organization, mechanics), content (e.g., APA style, use of reporting verbs), process (e.g., invention, editing), or psychological factors (e.g., confidence, awareness)?
- desirable impact—What types of changes should the program affect—individual (e.g., better grades, publication in professional journals), curricular (e.g., increased attention to writing in courses by faculty, common vocabulary for discussing writing), or external (e.g., improved graduate hiring)?

The next step is to determine a way in which the focus, orientation, or impact of the program could be determined to have been partially or completely achieved. This is how the goal will be measured. Educational **measurement** is an entire field of study, but measurement essentially involves the procedures for determining if a criterion for performance has been met. Typically what we specify in a goal statement is the ideal performance (or at least what would satisfy us) with respect to the focus, orientation, or impact of our program. We do not get into the details of how it will actually be measured. Some common examples for conceptualizing and specifying a performance criterion include:

- status relative to a community standard or benchmark *(an acceptable abstract as judged by faculty; at or above the 50th percentile on a norm-referenced test)*
- mastery of an end state (*consistent use of spelling conventions; ability to produce a coherent paragraph*)
- development relative to previous state (e.g., *increased use of citations compared to the beginning of the semester*)
- presence of a construct (*use of personal voice*)
- numerical representation of an ability (*writing fluency exhibited by producing 5 pages in 30 minutes; competency in basic English vocabulary shown by commanding 90 percent of 2,000 most common words*)

Note that many of these examples open up the goal to be measured in degrees or levels (e.g., no use/inconsistent use/consistent use; small/moderate/large increase; 1/3/7 citations per page), allowing you to examine both progress toward a goal and high achievement. Goals can also be worded as an up or down affair, meaning that they are either met or not met (e.g., *students will produce at least one draft before they submit a final paper*). When choosing which way to word your goal, consider what will happen if a goal is not met. Is it important to be able to show partial progress?

Also, generally we think of goals as something that the program will bring about through instruction. Some assessment programs, however, involve producing descriptive information for an academic unit. For example, a unit may ask a Writing Center to assess the writing ability of applicants to a program. In this case, the goals represent what the unit wants to know about what students can already do before the assessment (e.g., *the applicant shows creative use of language*).

Composing Goal Statements

The number of goals for a program will vary depending on the scope of the program, but three to five is often a good number because it allows for specificity without creating too much to keep track of. It is also best to make sure that all the stakeholders (e.g., partnering units, students, writing center, instructors) find the goals acceptable. One way of achieving the optimal number might be to make a list of goals longer than five and then ask the various stakeholders to select the most important from their perspective.

Goals should be worded in terms of the outcomes for participants. (Sometimes these are called SWBATs, for **S**tudents **W**ill **B**e **A**ble **T**o.) Statements about inputs or activities are not goals (e.g., *a website will be constructed, or students will meet with peer tutors three times*). A general template for goal statements is shown in Figure 2.1.

Figure 2.1. Template for Goal Statements

Students	**will be able to**	*active verb such as* : **create, apply, construct, translate, formulate, identify, solve, construct**	*product, process, or relation identified in mission statement*
	will know	*summary of content*	
	will be/feel	*description of a psychological state*	

Examples of goal statements:

Students will be able to create a concept map as part of their planning process.
Students will know conventions for common usage.
Students will be more confident about their writing ability.

Resources

Chapter 5 Worksheets

The worksheets on *Working with Example Goal Statements* and *Goals Development* (pages 106–11) will help you consider the types of goals that you might write as you begin the process of developing specific and measureable statements. If you have a planning group for your program, try working through them together.

Further Reading

Bloom, B., Englehart, M., Furst, E., Hill, W., & Krathwohl, D. (1956). *Taxonomy of educational objectives: The classification of educational goals. Handbook I: Cognitive domain.* New York: Longman, Green.

For more technical discussions of measurement issues, consult the *Journal of Educational Measurement*, www.wiley.com.

Huitt, W. (2004). Bloom et al.'s taxonomy of the cognitive domain. *Educational Psychology Interactive.* Valdosta, GA: Valdosta State University. Available from www.edpsycinteractive.org/topics/cogsys/bloom.html

An Internet search for "writing measurable goals" will also turn up many helpful sites.

Formative Activities

> Formative assessment "encompass[es] all those activities undertaken by teachers, and/or by their students, which provide information to be used as feedback to modify the teaching and learning activities in which they are engaged."
>
> —Paul Black and Dylan Wiliam, *Assessment in Education* 5(1), 1998

Ways to Enhance Learning

When assessing student learning, we draw principled inferences about current states and needs as well as the changes taking place. When we make those inferences for the purposes of enhancing the learning that is taking place, it is called formative assessment. There are three principle types of formative assessment serving different purposes:

- diagnostic assessment—analysis of student work and/or demographic information for the purpose of planning instruction or future learning
- feedback—immediate response to student work for the purpose of revision or as general preparation for future work; promotes critical awareness of strengths and weaknesses
- retrospective analysis—focus is on what has been achieved as a basis for post-program activity (e.g., life-long learning)

Since formative assessment typically evaluates student work, we often think of it as an activity primarily for helping students improve their performance. In reality, however, formative assessments can also benefit instructors and administrators for both the unit delivering the instruction as well as the sponsoring unit.

These scenarios illustrate the three principle types of formative assessment. They also provide examples of assessment activities serving multiple audiences. As you read them, consider ways in which all the stakeholders can make changes that will enhance current or future students' learning.

- **Diagnostic**—During orientation week, first-year students are asked first to complete a survey about strategies they employ when reading and writing academic material and then to read a persuasive article and write a response to it. Instructors in the first-year composition program evaluate it for grammatical constructions characteristic of second language writers, determine whether the student correctly identified the article's persuasive intentions, and decide whether the student's paper is a summary, response, or neither. The Director of the First-Year Composition Program examines the number of papers where evaluators noted grammatical constructions characteristic of second language writers to determine if an appropriate number of sections designated for multilingual writers has been scheduled. The instructors look at the results for identification of the article's persuasive intentions to determine whether they have enough attention devoted to reading skills and text analysis in their syllabi. During the first week of school, the students receive a handout from Learning Support Services that summarizes responses by college seniors to the strategy survey they completed as an indication of what more experienced students do. They also receive a copy of the essay they wrote along with the evaluation for article comprehension and target response. Then they are asked to identify three things they would like to improve during the semester.

- **Feedback**—High school students in an after-school enrichment program focused on creative writing are learning strategies for revising their prose to achieve different effects. After practicing the strategies with sample paragraphs supplied by the teacher, they are asked to revise something they have written and to share it with the other students by reading it aloud. While each student is reading aloud, the other students describe differences in the effect created by the original and revised drafts on a form with each student's name. The last question on the form asks the students to write one thing they learned from that day's session. At the end of the class, they give the form to the teacher, who makes a copy and then cuts it up so that she can give each student the portion that pertained to his or her work. The students are asked to write a poem expressing their feelings after reading their classmates' comments before next week's class. The teacher looks at all the comments for each student and records what percentage of the listeners seemed to feel the revisions were successful. She also checks off when a comment specifically mentions a strategy that she has introduced. The teacher uses this information to identify students who need more one-on-one work. She also uses the strategy checklist and the students' statements about what they learned in a weekly update for the school principal. The school principal likes to talk to students from the class in the hallway and compliment them on what they are learning.
- **Retrospective**—Students in the senior engineering capstone course have been required to attend workshops run by the Writing Center on abstract and proposal writing as well as effective presentations. Two consultants from the

> Writing Center have also been assigned to work with the students to help them prepare for the final presentation. The consultants are then invited to the class presentations, and afterward the professor invites the students and consultants to stick around for pizza and a discussion. The professor asks the department's administrative assistant to take notes on the discussion. The professor asks for comments about the effectiveness of the collaboration with the Writing Center, whether there should have been more collaboration, if it should have started in earlier classes, whether students could have prepared differently before meeting with the consultants, and how confident students felt about their ability to prepare a real project proposal in a job setting. The professor concludes the session by encouraging the students to always pay attention to their writing and to seek out people who can give them feedback. The professor shares the notes from the discussion with the Writing Center Director who includes a summary in a report to the Engineering Department Chair. He also keeps the notes to share with the consultants who will be working with the program next year.

These scenarios present idealized situations. Not every instance of formative assessment has to serve multiple audiences, nor do all three types have to be included with every program. With the program's goals in mind, you need to evaluate the usefulness of including formalized forms of the three types. Factors that may influence your decisions include:

- how possible it will be to change the program once it has started
- whether the program will be repeated
- whether the number of students involved makes getting a "big picture" important
- the degree to which instruction and learning will be individualized
- how important it is for the participants to be aware of their learning
- whether assessment activities are needed to help motivate participation

Resources

Chapter 5 Worksheets

The *Formative Assessments* worksheet (pages 112–13) asks you to begin by listing potential tools for gathering assessment data. Then it gives you a chart to identify which tools can be used for which purposes and audiences. It is not necessary for every purpose and every audience to be covered, but it is especially useful to consider how a tool might be used by different audiences.

Further Reading

Black, P., & William, D. (1998). Assessment and classroom learning. *Assessment in Education: Principles, Policy & Practice, 5*(1), 7–75.

Harlen, W., & Winter, J. (2004). The development of assessment for learning: Learning from the case of science and mathematics. *Language Testing, 21*(3), 390–408.

Huot, B. (2002). *(Re)articulating writing assessment for teaching and learning.* Logan: Utah State University Press.

Leung, C. (2004). Developing formative teacher assessment: Knowledge, practice, and change. *Language Assessment Quarterly: An International Journal, 1*(1), 19–41.

Summative Activities

> "Our complex, decentralized postsecondary education system has no comprehensive strategy, particularly for undergraduate programs, to provide either adequate internal accountability systems or effective public information. Too many decisions about higher education—from those made by policymakers to those made by students and families—rely heavily on reputation and rankings derived to a large extent from inputs such as financial resources rather than outcomes. Better data about real performance and lifelong working and learning ability is absolutely essential if we are to meet national needs and improve institutional performance."
>
> —U.S. Department of Education (2006). *A Test of Leadership: Charting the Future of U.S. Higher Education,* p. 14.

Accountability

When designing a program you need to identify the stakeholders—usually administrators, your supervisors, and the students themselves. They are the people who want the program to succeed but who also want some evidence of whether or not it has. Their investment may be financial, it may be time, or it may be moral support and credibility. Whatever it is, they expect you to show them what the program has achieved. Depending on the program, they may also want information about how this group of participants compares to another group or their mastery of a broader curriculum (i.e., have they learned what they should after 36 hours in the major?). If you want to make definitive and authoritative statements about students' abilities or progress, then you cannot put forward a series of ad hoc observations or impressions. You need to have a plan, which all the stakeholders agree to—ideally before it starts, for researching whether the goals of the program have been achieved.

As noted earlier goals specify a desired performance criterion or outcome (e.g., students will be able to produce a conference-quality abstract; students will show consistent use of a citation system) that identifies what you should be measuring (i.e., appropriateness for a conference, citation correctness) but leaves open the procedure for determining that the standard has been met. In order to determine that a performance criterion has been met, we need a baseline reference.

Several options exist. You can compare the students to themselves and chart individual progress. This is one of the most common ways to show achievement and is called a **pre/post study**. It can be problematic, however, because it assumes that all of the desired changes occur during the course of the program. In other words, if you adopt this approach, you want to be confident that there will be no lag time in understanding what is being taught.

A second possibility is to compare the students to the performance of an earlier group of students. The earlier group of students is called the **norming population**; this approach frequently employs a **norm-referenced test**, which is also referred to as a "**standardized test**." This type of comparison occurs when we evaluate a set of essays for placement purposes every year using a **rubric** and **benchmark essays** that illustrate the levels on the rubric. The benchmark essays, written by the first group of students to take the test, provide assurance that what was deemed acceptable in the beginning is still the same. (Note that this type of assessment is often combined with other baselines, as when we use the rubric to evaluate students at the beginning and end of the semester.)

Another option is to define the standards yourself. This is called a **criterion-referenced approach**. If we write a test that covers key elements of APA style, for example, we determine what those key elements are and set them as the standard for expected knowledge. Most classroom tests fall into this category.

A final option is to conduct an **experimental study** in which the standard is the performance of a **control group**, whose members are identical to the students you are assessing except that they have not experienced the **treatment**. In true experimental studies, the participants are assigned to the two groups completely randomly. Such a situation is very rare in educational contexts, and so usually we have to go with a **quasi-experimental** study in which we use intact classes and assume that the reasons students are enrolled in the two classes are roughly the same and that no inherent differences exist. For example, we want to make sure that a late afternoon class doesn't primarily enroll students with late night jobs while the morning class being compared primarily enrolls students without jobs. With experimental studies, we also need to be able to say in good conscience that we do not know whether the treatment is beneficial and whether denying it to the control group is unfair.

The ways in which the results for these different types of assessments are typically reported and the situations where they would be most useful are further illustrated in Table 2.1.

Table 2.1. Options for Summative Assessments			
Baseline Reference	**How Results Are Reported**	**Usefulness**	**Examples**
Previous performance (**pre/post study**)	**Statistical significance** of difference between pre and post scores	Judging immediate impact of instruction	• Survey administered to students at beginning, mid-way, and end of degree program • Writing sample at beginning and end of instructional program • **Longitudinal** tracking **study** that follows students for period after instructional program
Performance of similar group of students (**standardized** or **norm-referenced test**)	Comparison of number of students in different **percentile ranks** on test; statistical significance of differences between two groups	Locating individual within a group; describing change over time of student population	• New student **placement test** graded using **benchmark** writing samples and administered every semester • SAT®, TOEFL®, GRE®
Externally defined criteria (**criterion referenced**)	Percent of objectives achieved; pass/fail or refer/do not refer for additional instruction	Success of curriculum	• Classroom tests
Cntrol group (**experimental** or **quasi-experimental study**)	Statistical significance of differences	Judging effectiveness of intervention	• Paper grades for biology students who received writing instruction compared to students who did not

Resources

Chapter 5 Worksheets

The *Summative Assessment* worksheet (see pages 114–15) provides examples of goals and ways to measure them. The second page of the worksheet leads you through the process of defining your own goals and measures.

Further Reading

Haswell, R. H. (Ed.). (2001). *Beyond outcomes: Assessment and instruction within a university writing program.* Westport, CT: Ablex Publishing.

Kubiszyn, T., & Borich, G. D. (2007). *Educational testing and measurement: Classroom application and practice* (8th ed.). New York: John Wiley and Sons, Inc.

Yancey, K. B., & Huot, B. A. (1997). *Assessing writing across the curriculum.* Westport, CT: Ablex Publishing.

Resource Evaluation

> Had we but world enough, and time,
> This coyness, Lady, were no crime
> We would sit down and think which way
> To walk and pass our long love's day.
>
> —Andrew Marvel, "To His Coy Mistress"

Be Realistic

One problem inherent in systematic planning for assessment is a tendency to shoot for the moon. We specify goals that require detailed analysis of each student's work. We think of three or four different ways to get at the information we want. We are concerned about **measurement** reliability, so we decide that if two raters disagree on any one of five trait scores, then we will ask a third rater to look at the paper. We want students to receive feedback as soon as possible, so we promise a diagnostic assessment of writing samples from 75 students within two days.

An old adage states that any job worth doing is worth doing well. Assessment is no exception. The best plan is useless if it cannot be implemented. Therefore, one important step in the design process is the evaluation of the resources that will be required to plan, carry out, and analyze an assessment. Resource evaluation will be useful for the budgeting process; it may also be necessary to ensure availability of necessary staff and space.

Three principal types of resources should be considered:

- personnel—including the different roles, the staff responsible for each, and the time commitment required of each
- space—whether space will be required in addition to what is normally scheduled for the program
- time—how long will each phase (design, collection, analysis) of the assessment take

Resources

Chapter 5 Worksheets

The *Resource Evaluation* worksheet (pages 116–17) prompts you to consider the size and scope of your undertaking so that you can plan accordingly.

Writing a Plan

> "Writing is Thinking."
>
> —University of Houston Writing Center motto

Bringing It All Together

At some point it becomes necessary to sit down and crystallize your thinking in a formal plan that includes written descriptions of the goals, the formative and summative assessment tools, and an evaluation of the required resources. The audience for the plan may be just you, but in all likelihood you will circulate the plan among stakeholders for their comments and share the plan with a sponsor to instill confidence; you may even share the plan with students so that everyone is on the same page. Use the plan to help you figure out a budget and to keep yourself on task. If you have problems writing part of it, then that may be a signal that the program needs to be thought through more carefully.

Resources

Chapter 5 Worksheets

The *Writing Assessment Plan* (pages 118–20) is designed as a template for a document that will serve as a guide for an assessment program and that may be shared with stakeholders as appropriate.

Further Reading

Maki, P. (2004). *Assessing for learning: Building a sustainable commitment across the institution.* Sterling, VA: Stylus Publishing, LLC.

Walvoord, B. E. (2004). *Assessment clear and simple: A practical guide for institutions, departments, and general education.* San Francisco: Jossey-Bass.

http://wpacouncil.org/assessment-models—The Council of Writing Program Administrators has prepared detailed descriptions of writing assessments conducted on a number of university campuses.

CHAPTER 3

Tools

> Quality assessment depends on having good data to assess.

Types of Evidence

Chapter 3 features the tools that can be used to generate data and to guide *the inferences* we make from that data. Data are a series of systematically taken snapshots, all focused on what's going on in a program. The key to good data is having a system in place that ensures that the snapshots are representative (i.e., not focused on only one aspect or one type of participant) and detailed enough for our purposes. Researchers typically divide data into two types of evidence: **direct** and **indirect**.

Direct evidence provides a realistic, unfiltered representation of the performance being assessed. It may be a paper that students write, a test they take, or transcripts of their interactions with a consultant. Direct evidence further divides into two subtypes: **natural** and **elicited**. Natural data cover anything that would have been produced even if it weren't needed for assessment purposes (i.e., regular program activities). Elicited data have guidelines for generating the data, such as a writing prompt or a request to talk about mechanical errors in a consulting session that's being videoed. The trade-off between natural and elicited data involves deciding whether authenticity or comparability is more important.

Direct evidence is really just a record of what happened, and therefore it usually requires some type of **evaluation guide** that ensures that the analysis of the data is systematic. The guide might be a rubric used to evaluate a paper or a coding scheme applied to a transcript. It might also be a specific measure, such as the percentage of sentences without grammatical errors. Evaluation guides do not make the inferences for us, however. They do not tell us if a four is an acceptable score on a rating rubric or if a

10 percent drop in the proportion of sentences without grammatical errors should represent progress. They merely make the process of forming inferences easier by focusing attention on specific types of information in the data.

Indirect evidence, on the other hand, arrives in a pre-filtered format. Whereas direct evidence requires someone to analyze it and make inferences about performance levels or achievement based on an evaluation guide, with indirect evidence the inferences are made when the data is collected, often by the students producing the data or by someone observing them. Common tools for generating indirect evidence include **questionnaires, attitudinal surveys,** and **focus groups.** When students respond to a question about the most helpful part of a program as part of a focus group, their responses represent inferences about program achievements. With indirect evidence, the purpose of the data collection instrument or tool, therefore, is simply to record the inferences that will be useful for evaluating the goals of the program.

Collection Procedures

Whether we are gathering direct or indirect evidence, we need to have a principled procedure for collecting it. Some basic issues to consider include:

- *Who?* Should we sample every participant or choose a cross-section representing the constituencies that we think are significant?
- *What?* Is the data comparable from one participant to another? For example, we probably wouldn't want to compare a research paper with a narrative essay for the use of sources.
- *When?* Is the data being collected at roughly the same point in the program for each participant? Someone given a survey at the end of a consulting session may respond differently than someone caught two weeks later.
- *Where?* Is the data produced under the same conditions for each participant? In-class writing samples can differ dramatically between a 90-minute and a 60-minute class.

The four principal topics in this chapter are:

1. *Production Tasks*—common ways of generating and eliciting direct evidence
2. *Evaluation Guides*—tools to guide the analysis of direct evidence
3. *Indirect Measures*—instruments for eliciting people's inferences
4. *Database Design*—issues related to the storage of data in ways that facilitate analysis

Resources

Further Reading

Swing, R. L. (2004). Proving and Improving. *Volume ll: Tools and techniques for assessing the first college year.* The First-Year Experience Monograph Series No. 37. National Resource Center for the First-Year Experience and Students in Transition. Columbia: University of South Carolina.

Walvoord, B. E., & Anderson, V. J. (1998). *Effective grading: A tool for learning and assessment.* San Francisco: Jossey-Bass.

Production Tasks

> Any individual's writing "ability" is a sum of a variety of skills employed in a diversity of contexts, and individual ability fluctuates unevenly among these varieties. Consequently, one piece of writing—even if it is generated under the most desirable conditions—can never serve as an indicator of overall literacy, particularly for high-stakes decisions. Ideally, such literacy must be assessed by more than one piece of writing, in more than one genre, written on different occasions, for different audiences, and evaluated by multiple readers.
>
> —Conference on College Composition and Communication, "Writing Assessment: A Position Statement" www.ncte.org/cccc/resources/positions/writingassessment

Writing Samples

Guidelines

One of the most common sources of data for writing assessments is an elicited writing sample—one that is produced in response to an assigned task or **prompt**. Asking everyone to write in response to the same prompt promotes comparability of data, which can be very important if high-stakes decisions need to made, such as who should be referred to a program or whether a program has achieved its goal of improving student writing fluency.

Good writing prompts are ones that encourage students to relax and do their best. Providing detailed information as part of the prompt is usually the best way to achieve this (although it is important for a prompt not to be so long that writers use half their allotted time reading it). In general, prompts should:

- be germane to the interests of the writers
- simulate authentic writing tasks comparable to ones students have been or will be expected to complete
- specify an intended audience, even if it is a general academic reader
- provide guidelines about how much time will be allowed for writing
- make clear the purpose for which the writing sample will be used
- specify the criteria that will be used to evaluate the sample

Examples

The two prompts shown in Figures 3.1 and 3.2 (page 28) were intended to generate diagnostic data about students entering a graduate social work program. The first prompt was administered during an orientation program prior to the start of classes. At this point in the students' studies, it was unrealistic to expect any real expertise in social work, yet the program wanted the topic to feel germane to students' intended studies. Students were given an hour to work on the essay and told that it would be used to identify students who could benefit from receiving extra help on their writing.

Figure 3.1. Prompt for Beginning of a Program

The National Association of Social Workers' *Code of Ethics* under the heading "Social Workers' Ethical Responsibilities as Professionals" takes the following explicit position on plagiarism:

> ***4.08 Acknowledging Credit***
> (a) Social workers should take responsibility and credit, including authorship credit, only for work they have actually performed and to which they have contributed.
> (b) Social workers should honestly acknowledge the work of and the contributions made by others.
>
> www.naswdc.org/pubs/code/

According to the Center for Academic Integrity at Duke University, however, an increasing number of students at U.S. universities do not take this issue as seriously. Based on research studies conducted by Donald L. McCabe, the founding president of the center, the website reports:

- *On most campuses, more than 75 percent of students admit to some cheating. In a 1999 survey of 2,100 students on 21 campuses across the country, about one-third of the participating students admitted to serious test cheating and half admitted to one or more instances of serious cheating on written assignments.*

- *Internet plagiarism is a growing concern on all campuses as students struggle to understand what constitutes acceptable use of the Internet. In the absence of clear direction from faculty, most students have concluded that "cut & paste" plagiarism—using a sentence or two (or more) from different sources on the Internet and weaving this information together into a paper without appropriate citation—is not a serious issue. While 10 percent of students admitted to engaging in such behavior in 1999, this rose to 41 percent in a 2001 survey with the majority of students (68 percent) suggesting this was not a serious issue.*

www.academicintegrity.org/

Write a letter to the editor of your local newspaper in which you take a stand on the seriousness of plagiarism. As part of your letter, include a definition for what you consider plagiarism to be. You may also wish to consider how this issue affects both individuals and society at large. What are the rewards of acknowledging credit and the potentially negative effects of failing to do so?

Your response should develop and fully support multiple points related to the issue of plagiarism. Please use complete sentences and paragraphs (i.e., no bulleted or numbered lists) and adhere to the conventions of standard English for grammar, spelling, and punctuation. The paper will be assessed for evidence of an ability to generate and support ideas, the organization and coherence of the ideas, and the professionalism of their presentation. You may use the back of this page to make notes and help you organize your thoughts. It will be removed before the essays are assessed, however, so please write your paper on the lined sheets that follow. (Do not write on the back.)

Source: Created by D. Reynolds for the University of Houston Writing Center

This prompt was evaluated using a **rubric** that called for a macro-level decision about whether or not to refer the writer to the program as well as chances to note specific areas where the essay needed work. Students who were referred met with a writing consultant on a weekly basis. At the end of the semester, during their last consultation, these students were asked to write in response to a second prompt. The content of the second prompt attempts to draw on the expertise in social work that they should have developed during their semester in the program. It is slightly shorter in length, reflecting the more limited time available for writing. This second prompt was evaluated using a rubric that called for a macro-level decision on whether the writer could benefit from continued work with a consultant the next semester. That decision was ultimately made, however, by combining the recommendation based on the writing sample with a recommendation from the consultant who worked with the student.

Figure 3.2. End-of-Program Prompt
The Graduate School of Social Work has begun planning its new student orientation set for August 2005. Along with other information about the university and the school's academic program, the school would like to include statements written by two or three students from this year's entering class addressing the things they wish they had known or done before starting the program. They have asked you to write one of the statements and have suggested that it be approximately two pages in length. Remember that the goal is not to scare the entering students but rather to educate and inform them. Your response should develop and fully support multiple points. Please use complete sentences and paragraphs (i.e., no bulleted or numbered lists) and adhere to the conventions of standard English for grammar, spelling, and punctuation. The paper will be assessed for evidence of an ability to generate and support ideas, the organization and coherence of the ideas, and the professionalism of the presentation. You may use the back of this page to make notes and help you organize your thoughts. Your notes will be removed before the essays are assessed; be sure to use the lined sheets for your response. (Do not write on the back.)

Source: Created by D. Reynolds for the University of Houston Writing Center

Objective Tests

Guidelines

Objective tests may not seem, at face value, to be very useful for assessing writing programs. If the program includes the presentation of content material such as a style guide or grammatical conventions, however, these tests can provide useful information about exactly what students do and do not know as well as what students have learned from the presentation.

When designing objective tests, consider:

- content coverage—are the topics you want to know about equally represented in the questions?
- format—does the question format (e.g., multiple choice, short answer) reflect the type of access to information that you would expect students to have?
- grading—will you need to produce an overall grade or are you more interested in how students respond to individual items?

Finally, if at all possible, it is a good idea to **pilot** a test before giving it. Let someone outside of the program who has some knowledge of the topic take the test to see if that person gives you the answers you expect. If that doesn't happen, ask why the person answered the questions as he or she did. If the test will be used for high-stakes decision-making (e.g., the program was/was not a success), then piloting the test is extremely important because it is very common for two people to read the same question in different ways.

Example

The diagnostic test shown in Figure 3.3 (pages 30–34) was designed by Jennifer Wilson and Kyung-Hee Bae of the University of Houston Writing Center for a summer program working with international graduate students in an engineering college. The program format was a series of instructional classes focused on scientific writing and the production of a research proposal. The principal textbook for the classes was Swales and Feak's *Academic Writing for Graduate Students: Essential Tasks and Skills, 2d edition* (2004, University of Michigan Press). Because the syllabus for the course was closely related to the textbook content, they developed a diagnostic pre-test that covered key topics they planned to cover from the textbook. The format of the test questions also resembles that of the activities in the textbook. By calculating the percentage of correct answers for each section of the test, they were then able to determine which topics were uniformly difficult or easy for all the students and which indicated a wide range of abilities. Note that this test bases the questions on scientific texts appropriate for graduate students in this particular program. The test would probably not be appropriate for a similar program using the Swales and Feak book for graduate students in a sociology program.

Consultation Transcripts

Guidelines

Transcripts of interactions between students and a consultant or instructor can provide useful information about both participants and the program. Transcripts can reveal students' conscious awareness of texts they have written, their general confidence with respect to writing, and their goals for a particular text. They also can show whether an instructor gives students a chance to explain their intentions before trying to "fix" the writing or whether the instructor tends to focus on global or local concerns when reading a student paper. When a collection of transcripts is examined, it can provide information about the effectiveness of instructor training, whether generalizations can be drawn about issues facing specific groups of students or the difficulties associated with a particular assignment.

Figure 3.3. Objective Test: Science Writing Diagnostic Test

I. Fill in the blanks with linking words or phrases that enhance the flow of the following paragraph.

An overview of implantation contamination was given by Stevie *et al.*, but effects of energy contaminations on dopant diffusion upon annealing have not been investigated. The dopant tail profile itself is not significant if the contamination level is low. ______________, the much higher damage level coming from high energy contamination in the incident ion beam increases the transient enhanced diffusion of B more than proportionately, ______________ considerable boron diffusion. ______________ control of energy contamination is very critical to device fabrication, ______________ damage induced by energy contamination can degrade device performance further, ______________ by increasing leakage current, if the damage is not annealed out completely.

(Adapted from and reprinted with permission from Shao, L., Chen, J., Zhang, J., Tang, D., & Patel, S. Using point defect engineering to reduce the effects of energy nonmonochromaticity of B ion beams on shallow junction formation. *Journal of Applied Physics, 96* (1). Copyright 2004, American Institute of Physics.)

II. Decide whether you think the author of each sentence was presenting his findings as fact or as a tentative possibility. For those you think are fact, write an **F** in the blank; for those you feel are tentative, write a **T** in the blank.

a. _____ This experiment proves that PDE reduces B clustering and enhances B activation.

b. _____ The regulation of body temperature seems to place demands on the respiratory system, which exceeds the need for gas exchange.

c. _____ The magnetic field may affect both the velocity and temperature distributions of a conducting fluid between two parallel disks.

d. _____ By applying the techniques of PDE, sensitivity of B diffusion on energy contamination is significantly reduced.

Figure 3.3 (continued)

III. Read the following introduction from a physics article, and choose the best tense for each verb given in brackets. Then write the verb in the tense you have chosen in the blank.

Precise control of the ion energy distribution (IED) _________ [to be] important in a variety of thin-film etching and deposition applications. In plasma processing, for example, etch rate and selectivity _________ [depend] sensitively on ion bombardment energy, especially for near-threshold processes. The IED _________ [to be] determined by the difference in potential between the plasma and the substrate, as well as ion collisions with the background neutral gas. For radio-frequency (rf) plasmas, commonly employed in semiconductor manufacturing, the dependence of IED on control parameters _________ [study] extensively. For collisionless ion flow, the ion energy spread depends critically on the ion transit time through the sheath and the sheath potential wave form. Wang and Wendt _________ [report] a method to control the ion bombardment energy by applying a nonsinusoidal bias wave form on the substrate electrode, _________ [design] to result in a narrow energy spread. Coburn and Kay as well as Smith and Overzet _________ [show] that ion energy can be controlled by inserting a separate electrode into the plasma, and biasing that electrode to control the plasma potential. . . .

In all of these experiments, ions _________ [to be] extracted from a continuous-wave plasma. Under such conditions, however, even when the sheath potential wave form _________ [to be] designed to yield a narrow IED, the ion energy spread _________ [to be] limited by the *spatial* variation of the plasma potential. This in turn _________ [to be] proportional to the electron temperature, T_e. Thus, the energy of ions entering the sheath _________ [depend] on *where* the ion was born, and the spread of the resulting IED should be of the order of T_e. A way to further sharpen the IED _________ [to be] to extract ions from a plasma of very low T_e. In this work, an ion beam _________ [to be] extracted from the afterglow of a pulsed plasma. The electron temperature _________ [decay] drastically in the afterglow, with only a moderate drop in the ion density. . . .

(Adapted from and reprinted with permission from Xu, L., Economou, D. J., & Donnelly, V. M. Extraction of a nearly monogenetic ion beam using a pulsed plasma. *Applied Physics Letters, 87* (4). Copyright 2005, American Institute of Physics.)

Figure 3.3 (continued)

IV. The following sentences are taken from an actual abstract in the *Journal of Applied Physics*. The first sentence of the abstract is given; however the other sentences are out of order. Read the sentences and decide their original order, then indicate each sentence's order in the original abstract by numbering them 1–8. (The first sentence is done for you.)

__1__ We have shown that energy contamination introduced by deceleration technology, for increasing the beam currents available for low energy boron implants, can affect fabricated junctions adversely.

_____ Furthermore, we have used MeV implantation as a technique of point defect engineering (PDE) to control boron diffusion.

_____ Such contamination at a level of 0.1% can extend the profile of 0.5 keV B implants 10 nm deeper after a 1050 °C spike annealing.

_____ PDE can reduce boron clustering and enhance boron activation.

_____ We conclude that shallower and sharper box-like boron junctions can be achieved by PDE with sub-keV B implants with highly monoenergetic beams.

_____ PDE lowers the critical requirement for beam purity.

_____ Diffusion of B in the tail region has been reduced significantly and the boron profile is much sharper.

_____ A highly monoenergetic beam with energy contamination less than 0.1% is required for submicron devices.

(Adapted from and reprinted with permission from Shao, L., Chen, J., Zhang, J., Tang, D., & Patel, S. Using point defect engineering to reduce the effects of energy nonmonochromaticity of B ion beams on shallow junction. *Journal of Applied Physics, 96* (1). Copyright 2004, American Institute of Physics.)

V. For the following words, circle the meaning that is most often used in journal articles about superconductivity.

Report (verb)
a. To carry back and repeat to another
b. To relate or tell about; to present
c. To complain about or denounce
d. To be accountable

Find (verb)
a. To discover or ascertain through observation, experience, or study
b. To obtain or acquire by effort
c. To decide on and make a declaration about
d. To come upon, often by accident; meet with

Figure 3.3 (continued)

Significant (adjective)
a. Having or expressing a meaning; meaningful
b. Having or expressing a covert meaning; suggestive
c. Fairly large in amount or quantity
d. Having or likely to have a major effect; important

Limited (adjective)
a. Not excessive
b. Having only mediocre talent or range of ability
c. Confined to a certain space or time
d. Small in range or scope

VI. Read the following paragraph, then decide which of the paraphrases following it would be acceptable in terms of the American definition of plagiarism. Circle each item you find acceptable.

Original Source: The existence of static stripes, initially contentious, is now generally accepted. But quantum stripes are more radical and controversial. Members of the quantum-stripe faction hold that stripes are, in fact, always present. When a material superconducts, the stripes do not disappear; rather, a quantum-mechanical superposition of countless disordered stripe states forms (Fig. 1a), in such a way that the overall state corresponds to that of a superconducting quantum liquid. (Reprinted by permission from Macmillan Publishers Ltd: NATURE. J. Zaanen Superconductivity: Quantum Stripe Search, *440*, pp. 1118–1119, copyright 2006.)

1. Although most scientists now agree that static stripes exist, there is still much controversy about the existence of quantum stripes. Those who support the existence of quantum stripes believe the stripes are present at all times and do not disappear during superconductivity; rather, a state of countless disordered stripes forms to behave like a superconducting quantum liquid.
2. Although most scientists now agree that static stripes exist, there is still much controversy about the existence of quantum stripes. Those who support the existence of quantum stripes believe the stripes are present at all times, and that during superconductivity the stripes behave in such a way as to mimic a superconducting quantum liquid.
3. Although the existence of static stripes is now widely accepted, quantum stripes are still controversial. Those who support the existence of quantum stripes believe the stripes are present at all times, and that during superconductivity the stripes behave in such a way as to mimic a superconducting quantum liquid.
4. Although most scientists now agree that static stripes exist, there is still much controversy about the existence of quantum stripes. Those who support the existence of quantum stripes believe the stripes are present at all times and do not disappear when a material superconducts. Instead, they posit that the stripes form a disordered state and essentially behave like a superconducting quantum liquid.

Figure 3.3 (continued)

VII. Read the following two passages and decide which is a summary of a journal article and which is a critique of the article. Label each with an **S** or **C**, based on your decision.

1. _____ In the article, "Is Nanotechnology Dangerous?" Service (2000) dispels many myths surrounding nanotechnology. He explains that several fears people have about nanotechnology, like that it could potentially be dangerous to the human race, trace their origins to Drexler (1986), and he includes interview data from several experts that refute Drexler's claims. This data is very convincing because the experts quoted are all top scientists—including a Nobel Laureate—from major universities such as Stanford, Washington, and Rice. Service does mention, however, that public acceptance in the face of these irrational fears may be the biggest challenge nanotechnology will have in the future, and again, he supports this claim with convincing evidence from academic experts and the NSF.

2. _____ In the article, "Is Nanotechnology Dangerous?" Service (2000) dispels many myths surrounding nanotechnology. He explains that several fears people have about nanotechnology, like that it could potentially be dangerous to the human race, trace their origins to Drexler (1986). Service includes interview data from scientists at Stanford University, University of Washingon, and Rice University that refute Drexler's claims. Service does mention, however, that public acceptance in the face of these irrational fears may be the biggest challenge nanotechnology will have in the future.

Source: Created by Kyung-Hee Bae and Jennifer Wilson for the University of Houston Writing Center. Used with permission.

Be forewarned, however, transcribing oral interaction is a time-consuming process. Even a 10-minute recording might take several hours. The most basic requirement for a transcript is that it have a way of indicating who said what. Often a time marker (e.g., every minute or five minutes) is also inserted. More detailed transcriptions may include symbols for indicating pauses or when both parties are talking at the same time. Because oral language tends to be segmented differently from written language, conventions such as periods at the end of sentences and capital letters at the beginning are often omitted. For a detailed discussion of transcription conventions see Gilewicz and Thonus's 2003 article "Close Vertical Transcription" in *The Writing Center Journal.* If you have the resources to do so, hire someone like a graduate student in linguistics to do the transcription for you.

Remember also that transcription data is just like a piece of writing; it is not an assessment tool unless you have a systematic scheme for analyzing it. What you choose to code in a transcript will of course depend on what you want to know. If you have trained consultants to ask students for explanations and to let the student work out the issue first, then you might, for example, want to count the average number of words per **turn** as a way of determining whether the consultant or the student is speaking more. If you have encouraged the consultants to begin a session by focusing on how the paper is organized and the student's thesis before discussing individual sentences, you might code each turn for whether it focuses on organization, argument, wording, or casual talk. If you have told students that they must prepare for consulting sessions by coming up with a list of questions, you might simply look for turns where the student asks questions. Finally, if you are conducting a formative assessment to identify topics for the next consultant training session, you may code the transcript for turns where one of the participants appears frustrated.

Example

The transcript shown in Figure 3.4 (pages 36–37) is an excerpt from an interaction between a walk-in student in a writing center and an experienced writing center consultant. (The portions transcribed as xxxx were not intelligible.) Space has been provided to insert general comments about what may be occurring in a turn as well as codes that might be used for numerical counts of a particular feature or characteristic. Sample comments have been inserted that provide an interpretation of what is going on in the interaction and that indicate who is taking the initiative. The instances where the student asks directly for input have been further coded in the second column for whether the request is for help on grammar (G) or content (C). Typing up your transcript in this format is a fairly low-tech way that will allow you to code by hand. If you are going to be working with a large number of transcripts, you may find it worthwhile to invest in a software program for coding qualitative data, such as *NVivo* from QSR International or *Atlas.ti.* Such programs allow you to select sections of text and mark them with both comments and codes. They will then count the number of examples of each coding category and also pull up the selections that have been associated with each code.

Figure 3.4. Transcript Coding Sheet

Comments	Codes	Writing Consultation Session
S explains assignment		*Student:* xxxx are we supposed to do this paper—for that we have to write xxxx and look at all the data. Then after that—introduction and background come to a conclusion or recommendation xxxx.
C clarifies S's expectations		*Consultant:* Okay. And you just want me to go over it?
		Student: Yeah.
		Consultant: Okay.
S requests info	G	*Student:* The tenses and all, I'm not sure. And conclusion, what are we supposed to do? (Tape Restarted)
		Consultant: Okay, I just had some—
		Student: xxxx
Procedural		*Consultant:* Oh, okay, I guess I'll look over that real quick too. (Tape Restarted) Just a few things, like, when I was reading through here you used some terminology I wasn't familiar with.
		Student: Okay.
C begins episode asking for clarification of meaning		*Consultant:* Like when you say "amplification of three," is that out of ten or, like—
		Student: Oh, no, it's—it's kind of like if you have some signal xxxx amplification of three times xxxx
		Consultant: Oh, it—okay, all right.
		Student: And "red board" is that circuit board xxxx
		Consultant: Okay. And, let's see here. Like, when you said, "Amplification of three can be used in different consumer electronics like radio, TV where they need—you could—like radio or TV or, like, does—you have this comma here so it's like you're about to start a list here.
		Student: Radio or TV?
		Consultant: Yeah, like either one and or you can—don't use both. And then like "the of the amplifier system." It's just a typo but—Okay, so that gave me a better understanding of the decision here. You feel you have problems with it? Like you feel like you—
S requests info	C	*Student:* Yeah, like, is this okay or should I write more or – you know.
		Consultant: Well I—now going back on this, like, I understand what this is referring to the amplification and the red board. Just define that briefly just because, like, I'm not—I kind of assume that's what it was but—
		Student: Where in different—the xxxx

Figure 3.4 (continued)		
		Consultant: Yeah, like, do you mean is it the same thing as a circuit board, like—
		Student: Yeah.
		Consultant: Yeah, okay.
		Student: Its xxxx
		Consultant: Okay.
		Student: Okay xxxx what my product is. I have to—first of all I'm making vacuum tubes. And then, like, for making vacuum tubes I'm trying and testing different kind of making xxxx
		Consultant: Okay.
		Student: And I have made that vacuum tube xxxx but vacuum tubes in different size and it's bigger, but in my project its better to use vacuum tubes. Do you know what I mean?
		Consultant: Oh, yeah.
		Student: It's cheaper first of all, and it's good for xxxx
		Consultant: All right, okay. I like the—you know, the making the reference to, like, electric guitars and stuff. That's—
		Student: Yeah, yeah.
		Consultant: Okay, so—
		Student: Amplification, you know increase—not increases but, you know, like when you have to transmit something over one thing.
		Consultant: —distance, yeah.
		Student: Yeah, so it becomes a weak—weakened, do you know what I mean?
		Consultant: Yeah, I know what you mean.
		Student: So—and with the amplification—
End of meaning clarification episode		*Consultant:* Yeah, I got—I understood all that when I was reading this. You explained it very well. And so—yeah, I don't think you had any problem with your conclusion. Let's see—well what—let's see—
S requests info	G	*Student:* Isn't the tense xxxx is it, you know xxxx
		. . . .

Source: Adapted by D. Reynolds from unpublished research data

Resources

Further Reading

WRITING SAMPLES

Polio, C., & Glew, M. (1996). ESL writing assessment prompts: How students choose. *Journal of Second Language Writing, 5*(1), 35–49.

Reid, J., & Kroll, B. (1995). Designing and assessing effective classroom writing assignments for NESL and ESL students. *Journal of Second Language Writing, 4*(1), 17–41.

Reynolds, D. W. (2009). *One on one with second language writers.* Ann Arbor: University of Michigan Press.

Ruth, L., & Murphy, S. (1988). *Designing writing tasks for the assessment of writing.* Norwood, NJ: Ablex.

TRANSCRIPTS

Cazden, C. B. (2001). *Classroom discourse: The language of teaching and learning* (2nd ed.) Westport, CT: Heinemann.

Gilewicz, M., & Thonus, T. (2003). Close vertical transcription in writing center training and research. *Writing Center Journal, 24*(1), 25–50.

Thonus, T. (2002). Tutor and student assesments of academic writing tutorials: What is "success?" *Assessing Writing, 8*, 110–134.

www.ets.org/ > Prepare for the Test > Paper-based Test > Sample Writing Topics—The Educational Testing Service provides a list of 100 sample writing topics for the paper-based TOEFL® as a study aid.

http://micase.elicorpora.info/—The Michigan Corpus of Academic Spoken English (MICASE) provides transcripts of classroom lectures, student discussions, and various formal and informal interactions on a university campus. The transcripts provide examples of conventions for writing spoken language. The database includes at least one example of an "English composition tutorial" (ID: OFC301MU021) and also an "English Composition Seminar" (ID: SEM300MU100).

Evaluation Guides

> i. We value high-quality, ethically defensible, culturally responsive evaluation practices that lead to effective and humane organizations and ultimately to the enhancement of the public good.
> ii. We value high-quality, ethically defensible, culturally responsive evaluation practices that contribute to decision-making processes, program improvement, and policy formulation.
>
> —Statement of values for the American Evaluation Association, www.eval.org

Rubrics

Rubrics provide rules or principles for evaluating. When discussing writing the term generally implies a scheme for determining different levels of quality or performance. Rubrics fall into two principle types: **holistic** and **trait**.

Holistic rubrics ask the evaluator to make a single judgment about a piece of writing. The judgment may be represented as a number (often 1–6) or a descriptive label (*superior, above average, satisfactory, unsatisfactory*). Some description should be provided to explain what these level judgments signify and to help raters differentiate between, for example, a *superior* and an *above average* paper. Although the level descriptors usually refer to things that you might think of as separate abilities (e.g., *development, organization, language sophistication, and clarity of thesis*), the final decision is a global one. Trait rubrics, on the other hand, direct the evaluator to consider such abilities separately and to formulate separate judgments about each.

Some people argue that the choice of a rubric style depends on whether you believe that the quality of a piece of writing depends on the sum of its parts or is greater than the sum. Others take a more practical perspective, arguing that it depends on whether you need a more detailed conclusion than whether the paper is *poor, satisfactory, good,* or *excellent.*

Regardless of the perspective taken, there are several key steps in designing and using a rubric:

1. Decide what characteristics of the writing to focus on. Are you interested in general writing qualities like organization, development and support, coherence, and language control? Or do you need to focus on specific techniques that were taught, such as verb tenses in the literature review, citation format, and credibility of sources?

2. Determine how many **performance levels** you need. If you are making a pass/fail decision or deciding whether someone needs to take a particular course, then you really only need two levels. You may choose to add a third to allow room for a middle ground that would signal a need for additional information. If you are interested in building a more fine-grained profile of a group of students, then you might choose 4–6 levels for a holistic rubric. Trait rubrics often use a point system for each trait and then add the points from each trait to get an overall number. Trait rubrics can become troublesome, however, if too many points are assigned to one trait. If you make organization worth 20 points, for example, then you need to be prepared to explain how a rater decides between not only a 5 and a 15 but also an 8 and 9. Make the raters task as cognitively simple as possible.
3. Write a **descriptor** for each performance level. Raters will need a verbal description of a "5" that will allow them to distinguish it from a "6" and a "4." With holistic rubrics, the descriptors sometimes look identical with only descriptive adjectives changed from one level to the next: *A 6 paper shows excellent organization and creative language use. A 5 paper shows competent organization and error-free language use.* This technique for writing descriptors really seems to go counter to the notion of all the parts working together, however, because the rater must decide first whether the paper exhibits *excellent* or *competent* organization before proceeding to consider whether language use is *creative* or simply *error-free.* Raters often find it easier if there is greater distinction between the levels and if the descriptors show how the parts work together: *With a 6 paper you are able to read without being aware of how the paper is organized and instead are able to focus on the creativity of the language and sophistication of the ideas. A 5 paper may strike you as technically controlled but nothing really surprises or impresses you.* With a trait rubric, such descriptors will ideally exist for each level of each trait. To scale down the amount of information the rater has to keep track of, however, sometimes there will be one general descriptor for what a trait refers to: *organization refers to the sequence and flow of principle ideas.* Then the levels are simply denoted as *sophisticated, controlled, inconsistent,* and *no control* with the same level descriptors for all the traits.

4. Determine the rating procedure. At the end of the day, rubrics are an attempt to put into words what we value in writing. Value judgments are inherently messy, however, and steps need to be taken to minimize the messiness. At the very least, supplement the rubric with one or more example papers for each level. These are known as **benchmark** papers. If possible, use multiple raters and begin by training them. Talk through the rubric as a group focusing on definitions for constructs and qualities referred to in the rubric; then talk through the benchmarks and why they represent a level on the rubric. Finally, expect disagreement and have a procedure in place for handling disagreements. One possibility is if two raters differ, let a third person also evaluate the paper. If the third person agrees with one of the first two, use that score. If the third person disagrees with both of the previous ratings, then take the average of the three. You also can resolve differences by discussing the paper as a group and agreeing on a rating.

Holistic Rubric

The rubric shown in Figure 3.5 (page 42) was developed for a program that provided writing instruction to prospective business majors. Students with the lowest score on the rubric were required to participate in the program, and the rubric provided additional diagnostic information regarding the students at that level. Because the business college was interested in a more detailed profile of its prospective majors, the rubric was developed with four total levels.

The writing task evaluated by the rubric was a memo directed to administrative personnel in the business college containing suggestions related to a particular issue facing the college. The descriptive criteria associated with each level focus attention on content generation, organization and development, and use of language.

Figure 3.5. Sample Holistic Rubric

Assessment Rubric for Evaluation of Writing Samples

4	The writing sample demonstrates a particularly effective ability to generate detailed content appropriate to the purpose as well as the ability to organize and support it in an effective manner. It uses clear and coherent language and formatting that conform to the expectations of professional and academic communities.
3	The writing sample demonstrates a solid ability to generate detailed content appropriate to the purpose as well as the ability to organize and support it. It uses language and formatting that conform to the expectations of professional and academic communities.
2	The writing sample is uneven or undeveloped in its attempts to generate and organize appropriate content. The use of language does not consistently conform to the conventions of professional and academic communities.
1	The writing sample fails to demonstrate competency in basic writing. The writing sample evidences recurring problems with respect to the generation or organization of content and/or conformity to professional and academic conventions for language usage.

Students who receive a 3 or 4 satisfy the requirements for the Bauer Writing Evaluation. Students who receive a 2 may elect to re-take the exam once or sign up for a program of individualized writing instruction offered by the University of Houston Writing Center. Students who receive a 1 must sign up for the program of individualized writing instruction offered.

The checklist is used to provide diagnostic feedback for those samples that receive a 1 on the overall assessment.

Trait	**Student Should Work to Raise Awareness of Trait**
Displays sense of audience (e.g., appropriateness of forms of address, appeals to reader, presumptions about background knowledge)	
Provides sufficient detail and development of proposal	
Uses paragraphs to segment message and provide focus	
Displays awareness of conventions associated with business memo (e.g., lack of salutations, initial statement of purpose, formatting to emphasize message)	
Uses clear sentences that avoid unnecessary words or overly complicated phrasings	
Adopts a professional tone (e.g., avoids conversational or colloquial vocabulary, succinct)	
Displays control of standard usage (e.g., articles, verb tenses, word endings, agreement, sentence structure)	
Displays command of mechanical conventions (e.g., appropriate use of sentence punctuation, apostrophes, capitalization, spelling)	

Source: Created by D. Reynolds for the University of Houston Writing Center

Trait Rubric

The rubric in Figure 3.6 was developed for a **summative assessment** involving a **pre/post study** of project abstracts written by groups of engineering students enrolled in a capstone class. As part of the course, students attended workshops about how to write abstracts and worked with a writing consultant. The overall goal was for students to produce better abstracts. It was decided that this goal would be measured by judging the quality of the problem statement, whether all the expected components were present, and the use of language. By separating out the different traits the instrument provided both a retrospective formative assessment of topics presented in the workshops as well as the necessary summative information about student progress. The abstracts written at the beginning of the semester were evaluated at the same time as the ones written at the end of the semester by raters who had been trained using benchmark papers selected by the designer from the entire set. This allowed for progress on each individual trait to be measured by comparing the student group's score on, for example, the statement of a problem in their abstract written prior to the workshops with their abstract written after the workshops.

Figure 3.6. Sample Trait Rubric

Capstone Abstract Rating					
	Serious Faults	**Uneven, Some problems**	**Solid, No real problems**	**Stands Out/ Impresses**	
Statement of Problem or Objective					
No mention of context or motivation for project	1	2	3	4	*Clear why the project was undertaken*
Completeness					
Unclear what was done or shown	1	2	3	4	*Method, results, and implications addressed with sufficient detail*
Language Control					
Grammatical errors, excessive jargon, generic vocabulary	1	2	3	4	*Precise, direct wording; succinct*

Source: Created by D. Reynolds for the University of Houston Writing Center

Mixed Rubric

Developed for a **quasi-experimental study** evaluating the effectiveness of instructor training workshops, this type of rubric, shown in Figure 3.7, evaluates each section of a biology lab report separately and then also asks for an overall quality rating at the end. Criteria for each section are provided as well as indicators for each of the four possible performance levels for each section. The study involved a comparison of reports written by students in classes where instructors had received the training with a set written by students whose instructors did not receive the special training. Raters were not told which group a paper came from.

Figure 3.7. Sample Mixed Rubric

Biology Research Paper Assessment		
Paper Number:		**Levels** *4—Fully and completely meets objectives* *3—Adequately addresses objectives* *2—Addresses some objectives but not all* *1—Serious deficiencies with respect to objectives*
Rater's Initials:		
		Objectives
Abstract		• Summarizes briefly the objectives, methods, results, and conclusions of the study
Materials and Methods		• Provides details and explanation of materials and equipment used • Explains sequence as part of method
Introduction		• States in clear fashion purpose and justification of the study • Uses summary of previous literature with appropriate citations to provide context for the study
Results		• Summarizes findings (as opposed to presenting raw data) using labeled and numbered tables and figures • Uses text to highlight significant findings • Presents findings using objective language without interpretation
Discussion		• Provides an informative interpretation of findings • Compares results of present study to those of other investigations • Qualifies conclusions in a way that avoids overstatement • Addresses limitations and possible sources of error in the study
Overall Writing Quality		• Includes all required sections presented in correct sequence and format • Uses clear and precise wording to create an objective, impersonal tone • Controls grammar, spelling, and punctuation such that reading is not impeded

Source: Created by D. Reynolds for the University of Houston Writing Center

Observation Protocols

Most people do not like to be observed. As writing instructors, however, we frequently require students to share their papers with someone else for review because we know that there is no substitute for exposing a writer to a reader's reactions. We also know that it is helpful for students to be the ones doing the reviewing because it raises their own meta-awareness of the craft. Observations of teaching and learning situations serve the same functions. As instructors—or even learners—observations can make us aware of behaviors or techniques that we are totally unaware of. If we are the one having to observe, they make us focus on the art of teaching and learning in a conscious and systematic fashion.

Parameters

It is possible for someone to observe a class or consulting session and then produce a list of general observations or comments at the end. It is usually more helpful, however, if observers have some kind of **protocol** that leads them to focus on specific features or actions. Some common categories of information for observations serving formative purposes are:

- time management
- interpersonal negotiation skills
- use of knowledge
- accuracy of knowledge
- listening skills
- organization and presentation
- balance of topics
- incorporation of assessment
- adaptability

Note that it is possible to use an observation record for summative purposes. For example, you may observe graduate teaching assistants to see if they are implementing strategies discussed in their composition pedagogy course.

In designing the protocol, remember that it should be user friendly. The observer will either need to be able to make quick notes while observing or fill out a report from memory afterward. Checkboxes can be helpful for the former; keeping the number of categories small helps with the latter. Finally, leave space for narrative comments and encourage the observer and the observed to discuss the form together.

Example

The Observation Record in Figure 3.8 combines a record of what happened during an observation of a first-year composition course with a chart for recording general evaluations of specific pedagogical skills. In this way it provides both micro-level feedback to the instructor about the lesson and a set of broader inferences about the performance of the instructor. Remember, however, that observations do not have to focus just on the instructor. An observation record could be designed that focused on student actions such as questions asked and answered.

Checklists

Checklists direct the evaluator to make a series of usually low-stakes judgments. Because the judgments involve only two possibilities (present / not present), they frequently ask for a large number of judgments. This makes checklists especially useful for formative assessments, where more detail is better. It also means, however, that there is more possibility for raters to make mistakes, which is why they may not be as useful for higher-stakes **summative assessments.**

Example

The checklist shown in Figure 3.9 (page 48) was used to gain an overview of the general needs of a group of students who were scheduled to meet with a writing consultant one time. The focus of the consultation would be an assignment to write a museum catalog description of a work of art. Because consultants would not have a chance to get to know the students, the checklist was used to generate a general profile of issues faced by a number of students as well as an individualized report for each student. Note that the checklist is worded such that it provides a positive message about what students can do rather than highlighting what they cannot do. The checklist was applied to a writing sample collected on the first day of class that was designed to be similar to the catalog description they would be working on in the consultation. The task was to write a one-paragraph description of an important object in the student's home.

Figure 3.8. Sample Observation Record and Evaluation

INSTRUCTOR ______________________ **COURSE** ______________________

Interaction Type: I (Instructor Fronted) / I-C (Instructor—Class interaction) / I-S (Instructor—Student interaction) / S-S (Pair or Group Work) / S (Students working individually)

Time	Interaction Type	Activity Description	General Comments / Suggestions
9:00–:05	I	Told story about night before	Wish you had listed some goals for the class
:05–:10	I-C	Put next assignment on board and asked students what words meant	Good comprehension check
:10–:20	S	Brainstormed list of reasons why issue is serious	Students asked lots of questions—might have been good to model first
:20–:45	S-S & I-S	Group work brainstorming possible examples of issue	Make sure you monitor all groups even if you're working with one student; several groups were off task
:45–:50	I-C	Groups reported back	Group work seemed productive; nice to see how students elaborated each others' examples

Focus of Observation	Weak	Adequate	Strong	Comments
Clarity of Lesson Objectives	X			Students need to be told why they are doing what they are doing
Lesson Organization		X		Appropriate for task; wish you had showed text where example used to make issue serious
Time Management			X	Liked the way you gave students a 5-minute and 1-minute warning
Control of Content		X		Again, more examples for students would have made it clearer what you are asking for
Responsiveness / Adaptability			X	You handled the class discussions well
Provision of Feedback			X	Students several times responded to your question that now they got it
Other: (making learning explicit)	X			Need to do a wrap up at the end that asks students what they learned

Evaluator: ______________________ Date: ______________________

Source: Created by D. Reynolds

Figure 3.9. Sample Checklist

Art History

Assessment Checklist for Beginning of Semester Writing Sample

This writing sample provides evidence that the student has the ability to:

Ideas

_____ Identify a topic appropriate to the prompt
_____ Think analytically about the significance of an object
_____ Generate supporting content sufficient for a main proposition
_____ Appeal to an imagined audience

Rhetorical Control

_____ Craft an effective opening
_____ Use transitional expressions and logical thinking to make a text flow
_____ Express ideas clearly
_____ Organize a short piece of writing such that it has direction (e.g., is not just a list)
_____ Bring a piece of writing to a conclusion

Language Use

_____ Use effective and varying adjectives to describe
_____ Employ appropriate levels of sentence complexity
_____ Self-edit writing for standard usage
_____ Use punctuation to regulate reading

Source: Created by D. Reynolds for the University of Houston Writing Center

Quantitative Measures

When applied to studies of written texts, the term *quantitative measure* refers to counts or ratios that give a relative sense of different elements in the texts. Researchers use **quantitative** measures because they provide objective criteria for what constitutes constructs such as accuracy or sophistication. In addition they often can be at least partially generated by a computerized analysis, which lessens the potential for human errors. They may be especially useful for writing programs with goals related to language development or editing.

Common Measures

Table 3.1 details some of the common constructs for which researchers have used quantitative measures.

Table 3.1. Uses for Quantitative Measures

Constructs Measured Quantitatively	
Construct	**Common Measures**
accuracy	• non-standard usages per sentence • non-standard usages per clause
complexity	• words per sentence • clauses per sentence
fluency	• number of words in timed writing sample • use of words known to be characteristic of a given task or genre • number of different words per total number of words (type-token ratio)
vocabulary development	• frequency of words found on lists of words commonly used in academia

Resources

Chapter 5 Worksheets

OBSERVATION PROTOCOLS

Blank copies of the *Observation Record* and *Observation Evaluation* sheets are provided on pages 121–22.

Further Reading

RUBRICS

Hamp-Lyons, L. (1991). Scoring procedures for ESL contexts. In L. Hamp-Lyons (Ed.), *Assessing second language writing in academic contexts* (pp. 241–276). Norwood, NJ: Ablex.

Haswell, R. H. (1998). Rubrics, prototypes, and exemplars: Categorization theory and systems of writing placement. *Assessing Writing, 5*(2), 231–268.

White, E. M. (1994). *Teaching and assessing writing: Recent advances in understanding, evaluating, and improving student performance.* San Francisco: Jossey-Bass.

OBSERVATION PROTOCOLS

Spada, N., & Fröhlich, M. (1995). *COLT: communicative orientation of language teaching observation scheme: Coding conventions and applications.* Sydney: National Centre for English Language Teaching and Research, Macquarie University.

CHECKLISTS

Hodgson, A. R., & Bohning, G. (1997). A five-step guide for developing a writing ccecklist. *Journal of Adolescent & Adult Literacy, 41*(2), 138–141.

QUANTITATIVE MEASURES

Geisler, C. (2004). *Analyzing streams of language: Twelve steps to the systematic coding of text, talk, and other verbal data.* New York: Longman.

Wolfe-Quintero, K., Inagaki, S., & Kim, H. (1998). *Second language development in writing: measures of fluency, accuracy, and development.* Honolulu: Second Language Teaching and Curriculum Center at the University of Hawaii at Manoa.

An Internet search for "classroom observation templates" produces numerous examples that can be adapted.

For more help with quantitative measures, a number of websites developed by individual researchers offer either Internet-based language analysis tools or software such as concordancing programs that can be downloaded for free. For example:

www.lextutor.ca—Tom Cobb's *The Compleat Lexical Tutor*
www.vuw.ac.nz/lals/staff/paul-nation/nation.aspx—Paul Nation's homepage
www.antlab.sci.waseda.ac.jp—Laurence Anthony's homepage

Indirect Measures

Questionnaires

The terms *questionnaire* and *survey* are often used interchangeably. Here the term *questionnaire* is reserved for instruments that ask questions, while the term *survey* indicates the use of opinion ratings to identify underlying attitudinal constructs. **Questionnaires** can be used to elicit demographic information as well as respondents' formative and summative evaluations of a program. Although they may use formats such as multiple choice items or checkboxes that require respondents to reduce their response to a particular category, the greatest value of questionnaires often lies in the chance for respondents to put things in their own words.

As with any instrument, it is important to consider the questionnaire from the perspective of the respondent when designing it. For example, consider:

- length—How long will it take someone to complete? Will they be tempted to stop before they finish?
- wording—Will the respondents share your perspective of what a question targets? Do you avoid terminology or acronyms that they may not know (e.g., textual space, WID)?
- sequence—Is there an underlying rationale for how the questions are organized (e.g., past / present / future)? Does the rationale reflect how the respondents approach the topic of the questionnaire?
- instructions—Are the instructions for how (e.g., click to submit, hand in when finished) and when the questionnaire should be completed clear? Do the instructions give the respondents enough information about the purpose of the questionnaire to make them want to complete it? Do respondents know how long they will have to answer?

Examples

The questionnaire in Figure 3.10 was developed for graduate social work students to complete at the end of a one-hour workshop on how writing changes when writing for different audiences. It was used first to determine the students' satisfaction with the workshop and their evaluation of its strengths and weaknesses (formative assessment) as well as whether they had understood key content from the workshop (summative assessment). Because it is relatively short, it did not take up too much of the time allotted for the workshop.

Figure 3.10. Sample Workshop Evaluation Questionnaire

Workshop Evaluation

A. How would you rate your confidence to write in the field of Social Work?

Very Low	Somewhat Low	Neutral	Somewhat High	Very High
1	2	3	4	5

B. How would you rate the overall helpfulness of this workshop?

Very Low	Somewhat Low	Neutral	Somewhat High	Very High
1	2	3	4	5

C. How would you rate the overall effectiveness of the workshop instructor?

Very Ineffective	Somewhat Ineffective	Neutral	Somewhat Effective	Very Effective
1	2	3	4	5

D. From this workshop, I better understand the different types of audiences.

Strongly Disagree	Disagree	Neither Agree nor Disagree	Agree	Strongly Agree
1	2	3	4	5

E. From this workshop, I can better identify the audience of an assignment.

Strongly Disagree	Disagree	Neither Agree nor Disagree	Agree	Strongly Agree
1	2	3	4	5

F. From this workshop, I better understand how to tailor my writing to a specific audience.

Strongly Disagree	Disagree	Neither Agree nor Disagree	Agree	Strongly Agree
1	2	3	4	5

G. What was the strongest feature of this workshop?

H. What one thing could be done to improve this workshop in the future?

I. What additional topics would you like to see covered in future workshops?

Source: Created by D. Reynolds for the University of Houston Writing Center

The faculty questionnaire shown in Figure 3.11 focuses on workshop evaluation and was created by Kyung-Hee Bae of the University of Houston Writing Center when faculty partners for a scientific writing program began commenting informally that they were seeing improvement in their graduate students' writing as the result of a series of workshops. Since the faculty had initially requested the program, it was felt that it was important to gauge their overall satisfaction as a way of ensuring continued "buy in."

Figure 3.11. Sample Student Improvement Questionnaire

Faculty Follow-Up Questionnaire

A. What writing and presentation skills do you feel are important for your discipline?

B. Please describe any changes you have noticed in the writing and presentation skills or attitude toward writing of the students you recommended to attend the workshop.

C. Please describe any ways the workshop could be improved in the future.

Source: Created by Kyung-Hee Bae for the University of Houston Writing Center

Originally formatted for an online questionnaire emailed to all faculty members as part of a benchmarking study of undergraduate writing at the University of Houston, the faculty opinion instrument asks faculty both to rank issues of concern and to use their own words to describe the state of student writing. The questionnaire shown in Figure 3.12 (page 54) achieved a high response, possibly because of the ease of submitting it and its relatively short length. (For more details on the study, see L. Barlow, S. P. Liparulo, and D. W. Reynolds, "Keeping assessment local: The case for accountability through formative assessment," *Assessing Writing*, 2007.)

Figure 3.12. Sample Opinion Questionnaire

University of Houston Faculty Writing Questionnaire

To help us understand faculty expectations and perceptions of undergraduate student writing, please take a few minutes to provide responses to the following prompts.

To which college do you belong?

- ☐ Architecture
- ☐ Business
- ☐ CLASS
- ☐ Education
- ☐ Engineering
- ☐ HRM
- ☐ NSM
- ☐ Pharmacy
- ☐ Technology

What level students do you teach?

☐ Undergraduate only ☐ Graduate only ☐ Both

When you assign and grade written work in undergraduate courses, which of the following do you mark up, comment on, and count for grading?

1: None; 2: Very Little; 3: Some; 4: A Lot	
	Accurate factual content
	Productive and appropriate research process
	Editing effective sentences
	Organizing paragraphs to support a main idea statement
	Synthesizing, citing, and documenting sources
	Grammar and mechanics
	Developing the topic adequately
	Achieving the appropriate purpose
	Addressing the right audience
	Other: [Specify]

What words *[qualities, characteristics, traits, etc.]* come to mind to describe typical undergraduate student writing in your discipline?

What kinds of writing should undergraduate degree candidates in your majors be able to do on a routine basis? *[e.g., synthesize several sources of information, write detailed instructions, explain a decision concisely, etc.]*

Source: Reprinted from L. Barlow, S. P. Liparulo, and D. W. Reynolds, Keeping assessment local: The case for accountability through formative assessment, Assessing Writing, 12*(1), p. 56,*

The series of open-ended questions shown in Figure 3.13 were developed by Robert Askew of the University of Houston Writing Center for a linked course taught by Mary Gray; the questions were attached to the end of an attitudinal survey used to document changes in student confidence and meta-awareness after taking linked History and English courses. The open-ended nature of the questions allows students to nominate topics and suggestions that the instructors might not have thought to include in more focused questions.

Figure 3.13. Sample End-of-Course Questionnaire

End of Semester Course Evaluation

1. Do you feel that linking courses has enriched your understanding of both subjects? Please explain.
2. How do you feel about taking classes that meet once a week on Saturdays, and has it affected your learning experience? Please explain.
3. What was your greatest obstacle (academically, technologically, or otherwise) to completing your assignments? Please explain.
4. Would you consider taking a linked class again? Why or why not?

Source: Created by Robert Askew for the University of Houston Writing Center

Attitudinal Surveys

Many researchers believe that observable changes in student writing as a result of instruction take a long time to become evident and frequently don't appear until after the program is over and the students are asked to apply what they learned in an authentic context. (See, for example, N. Sommers and L. Saltz, The novice as expert: Writing the freshman year, *College Composition and Communication*, 2004.) This means that what happens during the program may be more internal and less obvious. One way of measuring internal cognitive or attitudinal states is with **surveys**.

Surveys as discussed here use groups of **items** to measure single underlying constructs such as "writing confidence" or "awareness of conventions for referring to sources." The items in the group are differently worded statements representing the same belief or attitude—in other words, the underlying construct. For example, these statements both target an awareness of revision strategies:

I know how to revise my own work.
I know how to evaluate and revise my coursework accordingly.

Frequently, an item group may also include a negatively worded item for which respondents would be expected to express an opposite opinion, such as:

> I do not think that revision helps my writing.

The reason for using multiple items is that it is very difficult to know how someone interprets a single item if we don't have items with overlapping content to use to verify responses. For example, students might disagree with the statement on "revising my own work" because (a) they don't know anything about revision, (b) they understand revision but they don't practice it, or (c) they don't think of what they write as *their* writing. If they respond similarly to the two positively worded items and give an opposite response for the negatively worded item, then we can feel more certain about the inference we make about their knowledge of revision.

Usually when we write a survey, we initially assume that our multiple items represent the same underlying construct, but this is something that should be verified based on the actual responses using a statistical procedure called **reliability analysis**. Reliability analysis produces a statistic known as **Cronbach's alpha**, and a well-written group or **scale** should have an alpha of at least 0.60.

When designing a survey, we need to first identify the underlying attitudes or beliefs that we want to measure. These might be explicit goals for the program or information that will help us understand the students better and consequently provide better instruction. Then we need to write items that will target these constructs. Usually at least three items per construct are needed, and five is better. Finally, we want to mix the order of the items from the different constructs we wish to assess so that the association between the items is not so obvious.

Generally, respondents are asked to indicate whether they agree or disagree with each statement using what is known as a **Likert-like scale** (e.g., strongly disagree / disagree / no opinion / agree / strongly agree). Note that researchers disagree over whether to include an even or odd number of choices on the response scale (cf. Z. Dornyei, *Questionnaires in second language research: Construction, administration, and processing.* 2003). Whereas an odd number of responses allows respondents to take a neutral position indicating no opinion on the item, an even number forces respondents to either agree or disagree.

Finally in order to make inferences about a construct, the response categories are assigned numerical values (i.e., strongly disagree = 1, disagree = 2, no opinion = 3, agree = 4, strongly agree = 5). Note that the negatively worded items will have to be converted to their opposite value on the scale before averaging with the positively worded items (1→5, 2→4, and vice versa). Responses to the items are then averaged. Thus if students answered strongly agree (1) and disagree (2) to the positively worded items and strongly agree to the negatively worded item (5→1), the average would be 1.3 (1+2+1 divided by 3). The mean response for the scale can then be averaged to produce a group average for the particular scale.

Examples

The General Writing Center Survey shown in Figure 3.14 (pages 58–60) was developed and refined over the course of several semesters by Robert Askew of the University of Houston Writing Center. It combines both attitudinal survey items with demographic and open-ended evaluative questionnaire items. Versions of this survey are used by a number of writing center programs and are now administered through an online format that allows for instant collation of results. The key for identifying the underlying constructs measured by the attitudinal items is contained in the item bank (see Figure 3.15, pages 61–64).

Figure 3.14. Writing Survey for the Beginning of Course

Beginning of Semester Communications Survey,
University of Houston Writing Center

Please answer all of the following questions by checking the appropriate answer.

Is English your most comfortable language for speaking? __ YES __ NO
If not, please indicate the primary language in which you feel comfortable speaking:

____

Is English your most comfortable language for writing? __ YES __ NO
If not, please indicate the primary language in which you feel comfortable writing:

____

Where did you graduate from high school?
City__________ State_________ Country_____________ Year of graduation_________

What is the highest academic degree you expect to obtain in your lifetime?
__ Bachelor's __ Master's __ Doctorate or Professional Degree (Ph.D., M.D., J.D., etc.)

How old were you when you began speaking English?
__ 0–4 years old __ 5–6 years old __ 7–11 years old __ 12–16 years old
__17+years old

How long have you lived in the United States?
__ 1 year or less __ 1–2 years __ 3–6 years __ 7–10 years __ 10+ years

Prior to this semester, how many semesters have you attended college?
__ 1 semester __ 2 semesters __ 3 semesters __ 4 semesters __ 5 semesters
__ 6+ semesters

Prior to this semester, how many semesters have you attended UH?
__ 1 semester __ 2 semesters __ 3 semesters __ 4 semesters __ 5 semesters
__ 6+ semesters

Where did you take Freshman English Composition I?
___ University of Houston ___ Junior College ___ Other University

Where did you take Freshman English Composition II?
___ University of Houston ___ Junior College ___ Other University

Are you a full-time (12 or more hours) or part-time (less than 12 hours) student?
__ Full-Time __ Part-Time

Figure 3.14 (continued)

How often have you done the following? Please answer: **(A) Often; (B) Sometimes; (C) Occasionally; (D) Never**	**Answer (letter)**
1. Proofread your written work	
2. Asked a peer to read your written work before you turned it in	
3. Received helpful suggestions about your written work from peers	
4. Worked on an academic project with your peers	
5. Worked on or co-authored a written assignment with your peers	
6. Gone for tutoring or a help session	
7. Asked your instructor for course-related information	
8. Visited informally and briefly with an instructor after class	
9. Seen an instructor during office hours	
10. Discussed ideas for a class project with an instructor	
11. Visited an academic advisor	
12. Discussed career plans and ambitions with an academic advisor	
13. Discussed career plans and ambitions with an instructor	

For each of the following statements, answer whether you:				**Answer (number)**
(1) Strongly Disagree	**(2) Disagree Somewhat**	**(3) Neither Agree nor Disagree**	**(4) Agree Somewhat**	**(5) Strongly Agree**
1. Communications skills are important for professionals.				
2. I have good writing skills.				
3. I work on group projects for class with other students.				
4. I meet students outside of class to study.				
5. I seek help on my writing from other students.				
6. I am able to express my knowledge clearly through writing.				
7. I am able to express my knowledge clearly through speaking.				
8. I am prepared for the written work required in this course.				
9. I am prepared for the group work required in this course.				
10. Writing helps me organize my knowledge.				

Figure 3.14 (continued)

11. I am a good communicator.	
12. I am open to criticism from others about my writing.	
13. I am skilled at working in groups.	
14. I am glad that writing support is part of this course.	
15. I can communicate complicated information to others.	
16. I am confident in my writing ability.	
17. Writing skills will be important to my career.	
18. Presentation skills will be important to my career.	
19. Group skills will be important to my career.	
20. Communication skills will be important to my career.	
21. When I don't have time to study or complete assignments, it is usually because of work hours.	
22. When I don't have time to study or complete assignments, it is usually because of family obligations.	
23. When I don't have time to study or complete assignments, it is usually because of recreation / partying.	
24. When I don't have time to study or complete assignments, it is usually because of illness.	
25. When I don't have time to study or complete assignments, it is usually because of boredom.	

Source: Created by Robert Askew for the University of Houston Writing Center

As a tool to help writing center personnel develop their own surveys, Robert Askew also developed a bank of items that could be used to measure a variety of programmatic goals and informational needs. Some, but not all, of these groupings have been **piloted** in previous surveys used by the writing center. It is important to always conduct a reliability analysis for each construct being measured.

Figure 3.15. Potential Survey Items

Assessment Questions: What do we want our students to know?

Outcome A: To understand the process of writing.

1) I know the stages of the writing process.
2) I understand how the purpose of an assignment dictates its content.
3) I understand how the audience of an assignment dictates the manner in which it is presented.
4) I have trouble with the process of writing a paper or report.

Outcome B: To employ better writing habits.

1) I put report or paper writing off until the last minute.
2) I seek help on my writing from others.
3) I know how to appropriately cite sources.
4) I usually outline my thoughts before writing them down.

Outcome C: To gain greater writing confidence.

1) I am proud of my writing.
2) I can communicate complicated information in my writing.
3) I am confident in my writing ability.
4) I have trouble expressing myself in writing.

Outcome D: To understand the role of revision in writing.

1) I know how to revise my own work.
2) I do not think that revision helps my writing.
3) I know how to evaluate and revise my coursework accordingly.
4) Revision is an important stage of the writing process.

Outcome E: To gain a better understanding of their own personal writing issues.

1) I know how to take full advantage of the strengths of my writing.
2) I recognize my weaknesses as a writer.
3) I can identify errors made in my writing.
4) I know how to compensate for weaknesses in my writing.
5) I recognize my strengths as a writer.

Outcome F: To understand how to access resources and services for assistance with writing.

1) I understand how to find resources to help me with my writing.
2) I know how to access services to help me with my writing.
3) I do not know how to find assistance with my writing.
4) I know how to look up the grammatical and formatting questions I have about my writing.

Figure 3.15 (continued)

<u>**Discipline Specific Outcomes—Engineering**</u>

Outcome A: To understand the types, components, and value of report writing.

1) I understand how writing reports can aid in the project design process. (scheduling, budgeting, analysis of data, & communication)
2) I do not understand the differences between the types of reports. (e.g. Progress Reports, Technical Reports, etc.)
3) I know how each section of a report has a specific purpose.
4) Report writing is a valuable process.

Outcome B: To understand how to present and explain graphical data in an effective manner.

1) I know how to effectively present graphical data in my report.
2) I understand how to represent information in a graphical manner.
3) I do not know how to explain graphical data in my reports.
4) I know how to create and use effective graphics in my reports.

Outcome C: To attain confidence in oral communication.

1) I can convey complicated information in a presentation.
2) It is difficult for me to explain technical information in a clear manner when speaking.
3) I am confident in my ability to communicate when speaking.
4) People understand me when I express complex material in conversation.

Outcome D: To learn about the style, forms, and format of engineering writing.

1) I am comfortable writing in a scientific style.
2) I understand how to write several forms of technical reports.
3) I know how to write reports specific to the field of engineering.
4) Report writing is difficult for me.
5) I understand how to produce technical reports in the correct format.

Outcome E: To know how to find information on scientific and engineering topics.

1) I know how to find information on scientific topics.
2) I have trouble finding resources to help me with my engineering assignments.
3) I understand how to research technical issues effectively.

Outcome F: To acquire skills necessary to manage a group and produce group documents or presentations effectively and efficiently.

1) I am comfortable working in a group to produce technical documents.
2) I know how to organize work for a group project.
3) I can organize effective presentations with other people.

Figure 3.15 (continued)

<u>Discipline Specific Outcomes—Linked Courses</u>

Outcome A: To achieve a sense of community among the students and faculty in order to ease the transition from high school to college.

1) I am comfortable asking the instructor questions about the course material.
2) I do not feel a sense of community with other students in this class.
3) I am comfortable doing university level coursework.
4) I feel there is meaningful collaboration between the faculty and students in this class.
5) I am more comfortable engaging in class discussions in a linked class.

Outcome B: To appreciate the interdisciplinary connections made in the course.

1) There are meaningful connections between the subjects of this course.
2) The opinions and views of faculty may differ depending on their academic discipline.
3) I do not see the curricular connections between these linked courses.
4) From my course studies, I see links between subjects across academic disciplines.
5) Linking courses reinforces the information I learn.

Outcome C: To acquire technological skills necessary for web research and publication.

1) I know how to effectively research a topic using the Internet.
2) I understand how to publish information on the World Wide Web.
3) I know how to solve minor technical issues I have with the computer.
4) I do not understand how to cite information and images I have found on the Internet.
5) I understand how presenting an argument visually can enhance its effectiveness.
6) I know how to construct a navigation system among the "pages" or "screens" using FrontPage.
7) I do not feel confident in my ability to publish information to the World Wide Web.
8) I have good computing skills.

Outcome D: To develop teaming skills. (End of Semester Only)

1) I have not studied for this course with other students outside of class.
2) I talked about this course with other students outside of class.
3) I worked in small groups in order to complete assignments for this course.

<u>Research Questions: What do we want to know about our students?</u>

Question A: How do external responsibilities detract from the studies or our students?

1) When I don't have time to study or complete assignments, it is usually because of work hours.
2) When I don't have time to study or complete assignments, it is usually because of family obligations.
3) I have a lot of responsibilities in my life in addition to schoolwork.
4) I have a lot of control over how I spend my time.
5) I frequently choose to do things on the spur of the moment.

Figure 3.15. (continued)

Question B: How seriously do our students take their studies?

1) When I don't have time to study or complete assignments, it is usually because of boredom.
2) When I don't have time to study or complete assignments, it is usually because of recreation / partying.
3) I take my studies seriously.
4) Completing my schoolwork on time is a top priority for me.
5) I always want to make good grades in all my classes.

Question C: What skills do our students see as important for their careers?

1) Presentation skills will be important to my career.
2) Communication skills will be important to my career.
3) Group skills will be important to my career.
4) Writing skills will not be important to my career.
5) I'm not sure what communication skills will be needed in my career.

Question D: How often do our students engage in collaborative studying?

1) I meet students outside of class to study.
2) I seek help on my writing from other students.
3) I work on group projects for class with other students.
4) I am not skilled at working in groups.
5) Working with others is not helpful to me.

Question E: How confident are our students in communicating?

1) I am a good communicator.
2) I am able to express my knowledge clearly through speaking.
3) I can communicate complicated information to others.
4) I often have trouble expressing myself.
5) People do not always understand what I am trying to say.

Question F: How confident are our students in writing?

1) I am confident in my writing ability.
2) I am able to express my knowledge clearly through writing.
3) I have good writing skills.
4) I am prepared for the written work required in this course.
5) Writing does not help me organize my thoughts.

Source: Created by Robert Askew for the University of Houston Writing Center

Focus Groups

A **focus group** is a guided discussion among invited participants. Focus groups began as a tool used by marketers in the middle of the 20th century to identify consumer preferences. They are now used extensively by politicians and social researchers across disciplines. The discussion is prompted by a moderator using a series of questions designed to bring out the participants' ideas and opinions (their inferences) about whatever is being assessed. Carefully conducted focus groups provide rich sources of spontaneous data that can be very difficult to gather otherwise. They differ from an interview in that there are multiple participants. This means that the researcher gathers not only the participants' answers but also their reactions to each other's comments.

Analysis

In order to draw the inferences that you need, you should keep a record of what transpires in the focus group session either by taking careful notes or preferably by making a tape or video recording. The record provides **qualitative data** that are generally analyzed using a process of recursive review and coding. The researcher, keeping in mind the broad research question(s), reads through the transcript, making notes about common themes and similarities among different responses. At some point a **coding system** is developed that identifies the sections of the transcript where these recurring themes occur. Once preliminary conclusions (also sometimes referred to as hypotheses) are reached, the researcher then goes through the process again as a way of verifying the conclusions. It also can be helpful if there is more than one person doing the analysis so that they can verify their inferences against each other.

Guidelines

Here are some useful suggestions for conducting a focus group:

- consider carefully the demographics of the invited participants and their representativeness of the target population
- use more than one group to determine if the same comments and opinions turn up across groups
- ask someone from the research team—in addition to the moderator—to observe the session and take notes about interpersonal behaviors and participants' kinesthetic reactions, which may reveal whether the group's discussion is being dominated by one individual and also whether participants may have unverbalized opinions.

- use at least two tape or video recorders in case one malfunctions
- keep the number of participants manageable—between 6–12 is generally good
- reward the participants for attending by explaining how the knowledge gained may benefit them; also consider possibly feeding them or giving them a small gift certificate as a token of appreciation

When it is time to analyze the results, there are several computer programs (e.g., *NVivo, Atlas.ti*) specifically designed for analyzing qualitative data such as transcripts. Keep in mind that the reliability of the coding process and the validity of the interpretations is just as important as with quantitative data (see section on *Reliability and Validity*, pages 80–82).

Resources

Further Reading

QUESTIONNAIRES

Bradburn, N. M., Sudman, S., & Wansink, B. (2004). *Asking questions: The definitive guide to questionnaire design—For market research, political polls, and social and health questionnaires.* San Francisco: Jossey-Bass.

Fumento, T. (n.d.). Issues in questionnaire design. *Evaluation Technical Assistance: Dissemination Series.* Champaign: Transition Research Institute at the University of Illinois. Available at www.ed.uiuc.edu/SPED/TRI/questionnaire.htm

ATTITUDINAL SURVEYS

Dornyei, Z. (2003). *Questionnaires in second language research: construction, administration, and processing.* Mahwah, NJ: Lawrence Erlbaum.

FOCUS GROUPS

Fern, E. F. (2001). *Advanced focus group research.* Thousand Oaks, CA: Sage.

On the Internet, www-tcall.tamu.edu/orp/orp1.htm—*Focus Group Tips for Beginners* offers an excellent overview of how to get started and issues to consider.

Database Design

> The best data in the world are useless if they cannot be accessed.

General Guidelines

An assessment study can very quickly generate an overwhelming amount of data. If you are working with data that can be converted to numerical values (e.g., essay ratings, survey responses, number of instances of a code in a transcript), then it is best to design a spreadsheet where the data can be recorded. Here are some suggestions for doing this:

- Plan to combine as much as possible into a single file; it is alright if cells are empty. You can combine data collected at different times if the instruments used to collect the data were the same or at least had questions that elicited the same information—just indicate the time the data were collected in a column. Note that database programs (e.g., Microsoft Office Access) allow you to create multiple spreadsheets and then try to link them. This can get tricky and confusing—keep it as simple as possible.
- Create a spreadsheet in which each row represents a unique **record**. For example, you cannot put scores from the beginning of the semester on one row and scores from the end of the semester on the next row because it will not be clear whether rows represent different students or different times. In most assessment studies, rows represent separate students and the data they generated (e.g., responses to a survey). Other possibilities, however, might be a study where each row represents a consultation transcript and the columns represent the number of times a particular code appears in the transcript, or a study where each row represents a different professor and the columns code shows characteristics of the class, such as the number of assignments and whether the professor used a class website. The first column should always be used to assign a unique identity to each record (i.e., an ID number).
- Represent in columns the data that you know about each record (i.e., row). For example you may have a column indicating when the data were collected, if collected over more than one semester; a column indicating which class a student is in; and a column indicating which exact task the student completed, if there was more than one possibility. In general, create columns for the data you are most interested in (e.g., essay scores, survey responses).

- Related to this, enter everything you know about the data into the spreadsheet because what seems insignificant now may be important later and it is easier to ignore information than to re-create it.
- Represent all data numerically if possible, such as assigning "1=brown" and "2=blue." This makes it easier if you need to turn the data over to a statistician.
- Keep track of what each column of your spreadsheet represents, both the data source and what the values entered equate to. The examples include a key created in a word processor.
- **Pilot** your design before entering all of your data. Enter a little and then try to run the analyses that you are planning.

Examples

A spreadsheet for a study where writing samples were collected from students at the beginning and end of the semester is shown in Figure 3.16. Each row represents the data from a different student. Because all the data from the student are in the same row, it is easy to use a formula to compute the change from beginning to end (cf., Columns I and J).

Figure 3.16. Pre/Post Study Spreadsheet Data

	A	B	C	D	E	F	G	H	I	J
1	ID	Prompt	Consultant	Semester	Begin Trait 1	Begin Trait 2	End Trait 1	End Trait 2	Diff Trait 1	Diff Trait 2
2	15M9G	1	3	20061	3	4	4	4	=g2-e2	=h2-f2
3	22M5R	2	2	20062	3	4	5	5	=g3-e3	=h3-f3
4	01F4T	1	1	20061	1	2	2	2	=g4-e4	=h4-f4
5	11F8T	2	1	20063	5	6	6	6	=g5-e5	=h5-f5

The key for interpreting the values in each column is also shown in Figure 3.17. Note that the **categorical data** Prompt and Consultant have been coded with numbers instead of words to make it easier for a statistician to work with them.

Figure 3.17. Pre/Post Study Data Interpretation Key

ID = Unique code created by combining responses to following questions

- On which DAY OF THE MONTH were you born?
- Are you Male or Female?
- How many letters are in your last name?
- What is the FIRST LETTER of the name of the high school from which you graduated?

Prompt
1=plagiarism topic
2= academic honesty topic

Consultant
1=first semester working
2=second semester working
3=third semester working

Semester
first four digits=year
last digit: 1=spring, 2=summer, 3=fall

Trait 1 (Content)
Possible scores: 1–6

Trait 2 (Mechanics)
Possible scores: 1–6

In a study with anonymous survey responses, students completed a **questionnaire** at the end of the semester with attitudinal survey items as well as short answer questions. Figure 3.18 (page 70) shows both the columns where the attitudinal items were recorded (B–J) as well as the columns with the short answer responses (K–M). Note that again all of the data except the short answer responses are recorded using numerical values. Also in the case of Survey 7, where the student only completed the beginning of the survey, the cells for the final items are left blank (i.e., don't enter a code indicating no response—this will mess up the statistician).

Figure 3.18. Spreadsheet for Anonymous Survey Responses

	A	B	C	D	E	F	G	H	I	J	K	L	M
1	Survey Number	Q1	Q2	Q3	Q4	Q5	Q6	Q7	Q8	Q9	Q10	Q11	Q12
2	1	5	2	2	4	5	2	1	5	1	I got a better idea of what is expected in engineering documents.	Mostly. The instructor did the best he could but the material he was expected to relay could have been formulated better.	Massively
3	2	5	5	5	4	4	4	1	5	1	Presentation—using PowerPoint.	Yes. I relearned how to structure my work before I write it.	n/a
4	3	4	4	4	4	4	4	4	3	2	It helped me organize my thoughts and comfortably place them into sentences.	Yes. Taking the time to proofread my own writing allowed me to increase my ability for future engineering courses.	It was very helpful. Every peer contributed a great to my writing.
5	4	4	1	3	3	2	2	2	5	1	The fact that I was able to revise and perfect my resume.	Yes, because I was well prepared for what is needed in an engineering paper.	Very helpful
6	5	4	2	4	4	2	2	1	5	1	n/a	Yes, this class has introduced me to the proper style and format for writing engineering documents.	n/a
7	6	5	1	4	3	3	1	5	4	2	Organizing presentations and preparing them.	Yes, it was the second time I had to write a technical paper.	It helped to find mistakes I didn't see before.
8	7	5	1	4	4	4	1				n/a	n/a	n/a

Source: Created by D. Reynolds from unpublished data

Figure 3.19 shows the key for interpreting the values in each column. Note that the explanation for Column G (Q6) makes it very clear that the responses to this item, which was negatively worded, have already been converted to match the positively worded items (i.e., 5 was changed to 1, 4 to 2, etc.).

Figure 3.19. Data Interpretation Key for Anonymous Survey

Survey Number = unique identifier generated by order in which surveys entered
Items 1=Strongly Agree; 2=Agree, 3 = Neither Agree nor Disagree; 4=Disagree; 5=Strongly Disagree

Q1. Teaming skills will be very important to my career.

Q2. I better understand how the audience of a report dictates the manner in which it is presented.

Q3. I have learned how to access services to help me with my writing.

Q4. I have learned from the course writing consultant how to better revise my work.

Q5. Communication skills are very important for engineers.

***Q6. I do not understand how a progress report differs from a technical report.**

Q7. How old were you when you began speaking English? 1= [0–4]; 2= [5–6]; 3= [7–11]; 4= [12–16]; 5= [17+]

Q8. How many years have you lived in the United States? 1=[Less than 1]; 2= [1–2]; 3= [3–6]; 4= [7–10]; 5= [10+]

Q9. Do you consider yourself a native speaker of English? 1=YES; 2=NO

Q10. What was the strongest feature of the workshops?

Q11. What was the strongest feature of your interaction with the course writing consultant?

Q12. In what specific ways have the workshops or your interaction with the course writing consultant helped you as a writer?

(* Values flipped before entering.)

CHAPTER 4

Reporting

> It's all about audience.

The Report Process

Reports of assessment activities take several different forms. They may be stand-alone documents focusing on a single assessment or on multiple assessments. They may also be included as part of a more general report that summarizes all the activities associated with a particular program.

Preparing the report begins with analyzing the data. This data analysis generally occurs in two stages:

1. Generate the findings or results. If the assessment involves data that can be quantified, compute numerical averages, percentages, etc., and run any necessary statistical tests. If the data is more **qualitative**, summarize key themes.
2. Consider possible explanations for why you got these results. It is important to be objective at this stage. Don't assume that your program is why you got the results you wanted; be willing to play devil's advocate. Having considered a range of explanations strengthens your credibility when it is time to make your ultimate conclusions.

The next stage is the initial "write up." Generally reports will have multiple audiences both within and outside of the Writing Center. As a result, it is extremely important to know your potential audiences. Consider:

- Do they want a broad summary or extensive detail? Which gives the report more credibility in their eyes—that you understand the big picture or that you followed a meticulous procedure?
- How much statistical literacy can you assume? Should you include **significance values** or just report **means**?
- Will they value qualitative analysis, or do they prefer strictly **positivistic evidence**?
- How would they interpret a discussion of potential shortcomings in the study—as an indication of your objectivity and integrity or as a sign of failure?

Written reports generally follow this sequence:

1. program description
2. statement of goals being assessed
3. description of assessment procedures (method)
4. a summary of principal findings
5. detailed findings
6. interpretations and implications

After you prepare the initial write up, it is advisable to ask a peer to review it for clarity and to make sure you have all your bases covered. Then share it with your internal audiences. The report represents not only your work but also your unit as a whole. After everyone who it might reflect on has agreed to the wording and conclusions, then share it with your external audiences.

Dissemination of a report is frequently a very political process, and the process should be as carefully considered as the writing up of the report.

- Is it better to present it to audiences one at a time or release it to everyone at the same time?
- Does the report need an executive summary highlighting the findings or implications?
- Would visuals (e.g., graphs on a handout or a PowerPoint presentation) be overkill or a useful complement?
- What questions should you anticipate from your audience?
- What is your audience's attention span?
- What future goals would you like the report to leverage?

Chapter Organization

This section of the guide addresses different topics related to data analysis and reporting:

Data Analysis—guidelines for working with quantitative and qualitative data including common statistical procedures

Reliability and Validity—ways to promote the reliability of an analysis and the validity of the inferences drawn from it

Report Templates—examples of reports for different types of data and studies

Data Analysis

"If all else fails, manipulate the data."

—Wise Guru

Types of Data

Generally speaking, the researchers work with two types of data: **qualitative** and **quantitative**. The distinction between the two rests on whether the data can be coded numerically.

Qualitative Data

Common examples of qualitative data used in the assessment of writing programs include short answer responses on a **questionnaire,** comments made during a **focus group** meeting, and impressions gathered while observing classes. These provide rich sources of information for making reasoned inferences that explore issues such as perspective, motivation, and emotional responses. If you use qualitative data, you should describe the heuristic process used to arrive at your inferences (e.g., reviewed notes, made preliminary conclusions, ran them by groups of students and teachers, revised conclusions). Even though you do this, it is still important to recognize that your audience will see the conclusions as susceptible to your biases and experiences. Therefore, it is also a good idea to provide enough of the unfiltered data for your audience to decide whether they would reach the same conclusions.

Quantitative Data

Quantitative data can be reduced to a numerical value, which then allows us to apply mathematical operations as a heuristic for making inferences. One advantage of converting information to numerical values is that it allows us to work with much larger amounts of data. It would be hard to form an opinion about whether a class of 30 students improved its overall general writing ability if we did not convert our judgments to some sort of numerical shorthand. When working with numerical data, however, it is very important to understand how the number values we assign are related to each other. Table 4.1 illustrates the basic distinction between **discrete** and **continuous** data as well as the further subdivisions of discrete data into **categorical** data and **ordinal** data and continuous into **interval** and **ratio.**

Table 4.1. Types of Quantitative Data

	Types			
Basic Distinction	**Discrete**		**Continuous**	
What different values mean	Numerical values correspond to judgment that the category applies; cannot have fraction of a value (e.g., 3.2).		Numerical values correspond to something that could be plotted on a number line because the relative difference between units is equal.	
Further Subdivisions	**Categorical**	**Ordinal**	**Interval**	**Ratio**
Defining Characteristics	Levels are unordered (2 is different from 1 but not more or less).	Levels are ordered (2 is more than 1).	Levels can be plotted directly on number line (2 is the same distance from 1 as 3 is from 2).	Values are relative to a common standard.
Examples	Nationality Gender Whether assigned consultant or not	Rubric levels* Responses to a Likert scale* Refer for help/ do not refer	Number of words in an essay Number of correct answers	Number of errors per sentence Grade point average
Common Procedures for Using to Describe a Group	Percentages Frequencies Modes		Ranges Means (averages) Medians	

* Note: Although scores derived from rubrics or Likert scale data are technically discrete data, they are often treated as continuous data, as when we compute an average essay rating for a group or the average response to a group of items on a survey.

Uses of Data

The collection and analysis of data serves two functions in an assessment study: **descriptive** and **inferential**.

Descriptive

When we report the percentage of students who attended all their assigned meetings with a consultant or the average change between beginning and end scores, we are using a mathematical procedure to summarize the characteristics of a group. We do the same thing with qualitative data when we claim that students generally expressed positive opinions about a program. Every assessment report should contain at least some descriptive information about the population being assessed so that your audience has a general sense of the population. For example, with discrete data include a table or graph showing the distribution of values. For continuous data, include means with their standard deviations or **median values** (a mean is the default unless a few outlying values excessively inflate or deflate it).

Inferential

The primary purpose for collecting data, however, is to allow us to draw some conclusions about relationships. They may be relationships between the content of instruction and student learning, students' previous experiences and current performance, tasks and output, or any number of combinations. If data are qualitative, we simply use a reasoning process to infer the relation(s). If the data are quantitative, then we use mathematical procedures to try to identify patterns in the way the data vary (the origin of the term **variable**). Statisticians approach the identification of patterns in two basic ways illustrated in Table 4.2. If you are not comfortable with statistics, then you should probably seek advice on what procedures to use.

Table 4.2. Statistical Approaches to Establishing Relations

Question	Common Procedures for Answering	Examples	Potential Limitations
When we sort a group of values according to one or more other variables, do we get groups with different characteristics?	Discrete Data (based on differences in distributions): Non-parametric tests (Chi-square) Continuous Data (based on differences in means): ***t*-test** ***F* test** analysis of variance (ANOVA, MANOVA)	Does whether or not grammar gets discussed in a consulting session relate to whether the consultant is a graduate or undergraduate student? Do students feel more confident about their writing at the end of a semester than the beginning?	Positive results do not necessarily mean that the right variable was chosen for sorting (e.g., what if graduate students who work as consultants tend to be linguistics majors?)
Is there a pattern to changes in one variable that can be associated with changes in one or more other variables?	Correlations Regressions Factor analysis Reliability analysis	Do older students perform better on placement tests? Which items on a survey do students answer similarly?	Establishing a relationship is not the same as establishing causality

Resource

On the Internet:

www.statsoft.com/textbook/stathome.html—*The Statistics Homepage* by StatSoft, Inc., provides a useful set of explanations for a range of statistical procedures. Even if you are getting help with statistical analysis of your data, you still should try to understand what the statistician has done and why.

Reliability and Validity

> Some people see reliability and validity as trade-offs because techniques for maximizing one sometimes minimize the other. The truth is, however, a finding cannot have validity if the procedures used to reach it are unreliable, and reliability is worthless if it leads to an invalid conclusion.

Reliability

Reliability refers to attempts to minimize chances that the inferences we draw have been influenced by anything other than what we think should influence them. For example, if we are evaluating a student's ability to produce a piece of writing that meets certain standards we want to ensure that the student had a chance to produce the best piece he or she could and that the judgments about the writing are based only on the standards. In other words, judgments should not be marred by the student running out of time, the fact that the air conditioner was not working in the room where the paper was rated, or that one of the raters really disagreed with the student's opinions.

In designing an assessment program, first think through anything that might unduly influence the production or evaluation of the data we will use for our conclusions. In general, every assessment should be biased in favor of the students. We should actively try to make the assessment meaningful and engaging so that students want to perform their best. We should also think about the conditions under which the evaluations will be made. If we are using raters, we should make sure they receive sufficient training, are fairly compensated for their efforts, and have a chance to take breaks and get food.

A standard assumption is that all judgments will be erroneous to some degree, and it is best to acknowledge this when we report them. If our findings are based on qualitative data, then we can simply discuss factors that might have influenced or skewed our interpretations. With **quantitative data**, a number of statistical procedures can be used to check on the degree of error in different types of studies. Some of the more common procedures are shown in Table 4.3.

Table 4.3. Reliability Tests for Quantitative Data				
Use	**Approach**	**Procedure Name**	**Question Answered by Procedure**	**Desired Values**
Survey or objective test responses	Internal consistency of items in a scale or questions targeting knowledge of construct	Alpha	Does distribution of values in one part of data match distribution in another part?	At least .60, preferably .80
Essay ratings	Consensus	Percent agreement	In what percentage of instances do raters give the same or similar score?	80%
Essay ratings	Consistency	Correlation	Do raters perceive an essay similarly relative to another essay, even if they do not give it the same score?	.60
Essay ratings	Measurement	Generalizability Theory or FACETS / Rasch analysis	Can the influence on the final score of a factor such as the rater or the topic or the day on which it was written be measured?	Measurement of different influences can be used to correct reported score.

Validity

Whereas reliability studies try to gauge errors in **measurement**, **validity** questions address whether we are measuring what we think we should be measuring. The key issue, therefore, is how to determine what we should be measuring. As detailed in Table 4.4, assessment specialists generally list five ways to approach this issue.

Table 4.4. Types of Validity Studies

Validity Type	Procedure	Example
content	Compare content analysis of assessment tool to an analysis of program goals or syllabus	Compare content of quiz given at end of a workshop with a list of topics that were covered in workshop
criteria	**concurrent**—compare to results from a similar assessment instrument **predictive**—monitor future results to see if they match present results	**concurrent**—compare score on essay assessment with grade in composition class **predictive**—verify that passing scores on developmental English portfolio have passing grade in subsequent composition class
construct	Rational analysis of measurement tool adequacy, usually by someone with expertise in the field	Share benchmark examples for rubric with discipline area faculty and ask them whether they agree with the assigned ratings
systemic (or consequential)	Study of the impact an assessment has within the context to which it applies	Distribute questionnaire to stakeholders in partnering unit asking if they feel students are better prepared since the implementation of a writing program for entering students
face	Study of what students and stakeholders perceive an assessment tool to be measuring	Add a question to the end of a writing prompt that asks if the student thinks the prompt was a good measure of the kind of writing he or she will be expected to do

Resources

Chapter 5 Worksheets

The worksheets on *Reliability* and *Validity* (pages 123–24) can be used by a planning team as part of a discussion of what should be measured and how to measure it.

Further Reading

www.languagetesting.info—Developed as a collection of resources for language testers by Professor Glen Fulcher, the site has a collection of video interviews on specific topics, including reliability and validity.

Reports

> Tell me and I'll forget; show me and I may remember; involve me and I'll understand.
>
> —Chinese Proverb

Final Thoughts

In many ways the "final report" commits the judgments made about student abilities and learning to stone; it serves as a lasting record of what was and was not accomplished and gives permanence to characterizations of students. The report may be read only by a small group of interested stakeholders, or it may also take on a life of its own, serving as a justification for any number of initiatives for years to come. Hopefully, the topics in this book will have prepared you to consider carefully the implications and consequences of reporting on a writing assessment.

Five Examples

This chapter concludes with a series of five examples taken from actual reports generated by the University of Houston Writing Center for different programs involving assessments of writing. Each report was written with a sense of audience—the audience's desire/tolerance for detail, their plans for future programs, and the issues that they are likely to consider important for their discipline. Therefore, the examples should thus be taken as just that—examples, not templates or ready-made products. Use the examples to help with designing tables, finding the right phrase for describing a procedure, or thinking about sections you need in a report you must write. The examples include reports covering an array of data types and study designs:

Example 1. *Survey and Questionnaire Data* (Figure 4.1, pages 85–87). This document was created for a linked English and History course program. The primary means of assessing program goals was an instrument that combined attitudinal survey items with open-ended questions. The report was authored by Robert Askew.

Example 2. *Rubric Data* (Figure 4.2, pages 88–90). This report presented the findings from an assessment of essays written by students in a graduate capstone course. The college that requested the study was concerned about its students' overall writing and critical-thinking abilities and asked for an initial baseline study that could be used for comparison with subsequent cohorts of students.

Example 3. *Focus Group Data* (Figure 4.3, pages 91–93). The example pages show the Table of Contents, introduction, and key findings for a formative assessment of student attitudes toward group work. The study, which was requested by an engineering professor, used four focus groups and was conducted near the beginning of the semester. The original report was authored by Koji Otsuka.

Example 4. *Pre/Post Study* (Figure 4.4, pages 94–98). This example includes excerpts from a report describing a program in which entering graduate students in a college were assessed at the beginning of the semester for referral to the program and then at the end of the semester for whether they should continue. Participants were also administered a survey at the beginning and end of the semester to gauge changes in attitudes.

Example 5. *Experimental Study* (Figure 4.5, pages 99–100). This report summarizes a quasi-experimental study evaluating the combined effectiveness of a series of interventions designed to improve the quality of lab reports produced by students in a biology class.

Figure 4.1. Survey and Questionnaire Data (Example Report 1)

Survey Assessment Summary
English & History Linked Courses
Fall 2004

As part of the Weekend University program at the University of Houston, the Writing Center collaborated with faculty from the History Department and the College of Education on a linked course offered in the Fall semester of 2004. Students enrolled in the program attended a History section followed by an English class session devoted to writing. Students who completed the program received credit for both HIST 1377 and either ENGL 1303, ENGL 1304, or ENGL 2321.

Academic goals for the program included recognition of the importance of collaboration, acquisition of technological skills necessary for university-level research and publication, and gaining a better understanding of personal writing issues. At the end of the semester, the participants were administered a survey to assess their attitudes and beliefs concerning items related to these goals. Of the 60 students that finished the course, 52 completed the survey.

An analysis of the survey responses suggests that students associated the items on the survey with one of three general orientations toward the course: mastery of academic skills, importance of collaboration, and their personal understanding of writing.

- By the end of the semester, the students agreed that they had mastered the academic skills emphasized in the course as reflected in a mean score of 1.67 on the five point scale (1 = Strongly Agree).
- The participants also recognized the importance of collaboration in the course and across disciplines. This is reflected in a mean score of 1.71 on the five point scale (1 = Strongly Agree).
- Concerning personal writing issues, the students agreed that they had an understanding of their strengths and weaknesses and how to tailor their writing accordingly, as reflected in a mean score of 2.02 on a five point scale (1 = Strongly Agree).

Figure 4.1. (continued)

Table 1 illustrates the mean score for the items that associated with each orientation and the reliability coefficients for each set of survey items.

Table 1: Orientations to Course Sorted by Strength of Agreement

Orientations to Course	Mean score (1=Strong Agreement, 5=Strong Disagreement)	Reliability Coefficient (Cronbach's Alpha)
Mastery of Academic Skills	1.67	.84
I know how to effectively research a topic using the Internet.		
I am comfortable doing university level coursework.		
I have good computing skills.		
I know how to appropriately cite sources.		
I understand how to publish information on the World Wide Web.		
I do not understand how to cite information and images I have found on the Internet.*		
Importance of Collaboration	1.71	.79
I feel there was meaningful collaboration between the faculty and students in this class.		
I am more comfortable engaging in class discussions in a linked class.		
I do not see the curricular connections between these linked courses.*		
Linking courses reinforces the information I learn.		
I see links between subjects across academic disciplines		
Personal Understanding of Writing	2.02	.90
I understand how presenting an argument visually can enhance its effectiveness.		
I know how to emphasize the strengths of my writing.		
I can identify errors made in my writing.		
I know how to compensate for weaknesses in my writing.		

* Responses to these negatively worded items were recoded before the mean response was calculated with 5 being recoded as 1 and 4 as 2.

Figure 4.1. (continued)

Short Answer Analysis

Benefits of Linking Courses

When prompted to elaborate on how linking the courses affected their learning, over 75 percent of the students stated that linking the courses enriched their understanding of both subjects. Some students elaborated further:

> By linking courses I am allowed the opportunity to more effectively group together the things I learn to the way I can use them to better myself. Linking courses strengthens the curriculum of each course involved and helps me to retain and extract what I learn more effectively.

Another student commented,

> [I]n regular English classes, the papers normally are just random topics. In this class, you learn something in history and then go visit a museum and then turn around and write about it. You get to experience your topic.

Other students stated that linking the courses enhanced student collaboration and required a greater level of research.

Saturday Meetings

According to 70 percent of the students, meeting once a week on Saturday was convenient. Many expressed that the Saturday class helped them balance other demands with school. One student offered the following:

> It has helped me to balance my work (professional) life and my school life. This Saturday class has allowed me to work normal hours and have my nights set aside for my family.

Another 12 percent stated that Saturdays were not their preferred day for class, but they did prefer meeting for class once a week. Some mentioned other conveniences such as less traffic and more available parking.

Obstacles to Learning

The students were prompted for the greatest obstacle to completing course assignments, and there was no consensus among the responses. Many mentioned technological difficulties, as some of the students did not have computers at home or owned incompatible software. Others mentioned difficulty finding time during the week to complete assignments while trying to balance competing personal concerns.

Future Linked-Course Offerings

Approximately 80 percent of the students stated that they would consider taking a linked class again. Other students stated that they would as well if it were offered at a time other than the weekend. One student summarized, "I appreciated the one-on-one help, the weekly emails from professors; it just made things so much easier. This is one class I would recommend to others as well."

Source: Written by Robert Askew for the University of Houston Writing Center. Used with permission.

Figure 4.2. Rubric Data (Example Report 2)

Baseline Writing Assessment

Project Description

At the request of the Director of Assessment and Accreditation Services in the XXX College, the UH Writing Center developed rubrics that could be used to assess communication and critical-thinking learning goals for students enrolled in the XXX program. Additionally a baseline set of papers were rated for the purposes of providing initial data on student writing skills that could be compared to the performance of future cohorts.

Rubric Development

Following the template used for assessment of other learning goals in the college, three traits were specified for each goal. The traits specified for communication included:

- appropriate use of grammar and mechanics,
- appropriate vocabulary choice, and
- effective organization.

The traits specified for the critical thinking goal :

- analysis of the issue,
- clarity of the recommendation, and
- development of support for the recommendation.

The rubrics also provide descriptors for three levels of student performance on each trait: exceeded expectations (3), met expectations (2), and did not meet expectations (1).

A paper was categorized as meeting expectations for the learning goal if the sum of the trait scores was six. Scores below six were categorized as not meeting expectations, and above six as exceeding expectations.

The rubrics for each goal were developed by a tenured faculty member associated with the Writing Center and with expertise in writing assessment. They were also shared with faculty teaching in the XXX program prior to their use in rating the sample papers.

Rating of Pilot Sample

The baseline paper set was produced by students as an assignment in a required capstone course for the XXX program. The task required students to write a memo to the college's Director of Graduate Studies recommending whether or not UH should develop specialist XXX programs. As background to the writing task, students were given a recent article describing the development of such programs at various institutions across the U.S. A total of 49 papers were submitted for the sample.

Each paper was read by two readers—the faculty member who developed the rubrics and a graduate student employed by the Writing Center. In cases where the two raters disagreed on whether or not a paper met expectations for either the communication goal or the critical thinking goal as a whole, the papers were read by a third reader to ensure reliability.

Figure 4.2 (continued)

Tables 1 and 2 provide breakdowns for the number of students meeting expectations for each of the traits on the two learning goals. With respect to the communication goals, students performed best in the area of organization with 36 of 49 students (73 percent) meeting or exceeding expectations. The weakest areas were control of syntax and mechanics and the use of appropriate vocabulary with 35 percent failing to meet expectations for each trait.

Table 1: Summary of Communication Trait Performance (N=49)

	Student controls conventions for syntax, spelling, and mechanics.	Student uses vocabulary that is appropriate to the audience and form of communication.	Student organizes ideas and utilizes transitional expressions to achieve clarity and precision.
Did not meet expectations	17	17	13
Met Expectations	26	27	30
Exceeded Expectations	6	5	6

In the area of critical thinking, the strongest area was analysis of the issue with 39 students (80 percent) meeting or exceeding expectations; the weakest area was the development and support of ideas for which 19 students (39 percent) did not meet expectations.

Table 2: Summary of Critical-Thinking Trait Performance (N=49)

	Student analyzes issue and identifies at least two perspectives on issue.	Student recommends a clear and appropriate course of action.	Student supports recommendation with logical and developed argumentation.
Did not meet expectations	10	9	19
Met Expectations	35	32	21
Exceeded Expectations	4	8	9

While the results shown in Tables 1 and 2 indicate that the range of students meeting or exceeding expectations is between 65 and 82 percent, the percent of students who met expectations for all three traits on each goal is less. Table 3 provides a summary of the number of students who met expectations overall for the two learning goals. As shown, approximately 51 percent of the students failed to meet expectations (i.e., the sum of the trait scores was less than six), 33 percent met expectations, and 16 percent exceeded expectations.

Figure 4.2 (continued)

Table 3: Summary of Learning Goal Performance (N=49)		
	Communications	**Critical Thinking**
Did not meet expectations [a]	25	26
Met expectations [b]	16	14
Exceeded expectations [c]	8	9

[a] Sum of trait scores = 3–5
[b] Sum of trait scores = 6
[c] Sum of trait scores = 7–9

These results serve as a useful baseline for comparison with future cohorts.

Source: Written by D. Reynolds for the University of Houston Writing Center

Figure 4.3. Focus Group Data (Example Report 3)

Focus Group Study: Course XXXX
Assessing Student Attitudes of Group Work

Table of Contents

INTRODUCTION

Background and Theory

Four exploratory beginning-of-semester focus groups were conducted with students of engineering as part one of a two-part (entrance and exit) study. The study was intended to acquire data to implement Dr. X's overall initiative of "improving the 'group experience' for students in XXXX" since the course required extensive group work.

Figure 4.3 (continued)

The study had the following basic objectives:

- Assess student beliefs/attitudes concerning group work for class "team project."
- Collect qualitative data from the student's perspective—described in the students' own voice.
- Provide recommendations concerning the method of forming groups (i.e., students' choice, proximity, time scheduling, random).

As part two of this study, end-of-semester focus groups will also be conducted to elaborate the overall experience of group work in XXXX, as well as to document specific instances of conflict and how they may (or may not) have been resolved.

From the perspective of course assessment, focus groups are useful to the extent that they can yield qualitative data that supplement quantitative methods of data collection. Whereas traditional methods of assessment (such as exams) can test students on their knowledge or performance, they are not suitable for documenting students' reflections—that is to say, they do little to describe or explain students' attitudes and beliefs about their own knowledge or performance. Similarly, quantitative assessment methods (e.g., surveys and statistical analyses of demographics, test scores, project grades, etc.) tend to concentrate on the question of "what," "how many," and "to what degree." This emphasis on identifying and counting particular constructs can provide an incomplete picture at times. In contrast, qualitative methods (such as focus group discussions, interviews, and participant observation) aim to serve a more explanatory function. Questions are set up to find out the "how" and "why." In service of this explanatory function, focus group studies strive to provide a more-or-less open-ended arena in which students can conceive of topics in a flexible way that is more relevant to their understanding.

It is worth noting that an "observer effect" can emerge from this type of study: the method of study (focus group discussions) affected the outcome (student beliefs/attitudes). It was not unusual for students' beliefs and attitudes to shift—sometimes reverse—through participation in open-ended discussions during the focus groups. This led to two immediate consequences with opposing implications. One, focus groups cannot purport to be a value-neutral study that is completely separate from the subject it studies. Two, in this way, focus groups are not only useful as a means to supplement quantitative data, but also as a way to supplement the pedagogical objectives of the class.

Figure 4.3 (continued)

KEY FINDINGS

Key findings were derived by carefully analyzing the frequency, extensiveness, emotion, and specificity of comments made during the focus group.

- Students are aware that working in groups is an important aspect of their education as engineers. They understand that a career in mechanical engineering will require them to work effectively in groups not of their choosing (assigned groups). Thus, regardless of whether they could choose their own teams, all of the students believed that working in groups would be a valuable experience.
- Only one of the 19 students elected the hypothetical choice of working alone to avoid the problems of working in groups. All others agreed that working in groups would increase the quality of the product. Reported benefits of working in groups included the following: development of team attitude, communication, negotiation, and planning skills. The student who preferred to work alone was skilled with machine tools and had access to a shop.
- Participant opinion was largely split on the hypothetical choice of being able to choose their group members. Regardless of the preference to choose, all participants agreed that a lot could be learned by working with assigned groups. Those who preferred to choose their own group believed that being able to choose would increase the chance that "slackers" would be avoided, resulting in a higher group grade. One group in particular showed a dramatic reversal in attitude over whether groups should be assigned or chosen. Some of the members were surprised to see themselves contradict earlier statements they made by arguing *for* assigned groups. This change occurred after discussing the potential gain in "real world" experience by resolving group conflicts.
- Two participants believed that they would not be able to work with someone that they disliked. All others agreed that they would be able to "put aside" personal differences and work toward a common goal.
- Lack of familiarity with other classmates comprised a great portion of the anxiety or concern related to group work. Many students wanted more opportunities for classmates to interact in class, before the formation of groups. Most groups showed positive interest in the MBTI and questioned why it was not administered in the beginning of the semester. Many students felt that the self-introduction in class made them feel "on the spot." They questioned how much one could gain familiarity with others through such a brief and "forced" exercise.
- Through dialog in the focus group, participants acquired a more balanced sense of the difficulties involved in both assigning groups and choosing groups. The discussion often progressed with students offering contradictory points to consider the pros and cons of both ways.

Source: Written by Koji Otsuka for the University of Houston Writing Center. Used with permission.

Figure 4.4. Pre/Post Data (Example Report 4)

Introduction

The following report describes the first semester (Fall 2004) of a program of supplemental writing instruction offered by the UH Writing Center for students in XXX College. The general goal of the program was to support the development of academic writing abilities by students. Following an initial assessment of all entering first-year students, 100 students (out of 146) were referred to the Writing Center to work on an individual basis with an experienced writing consultant.

The students were expected to meet with their assigned consultant for 30 minutes per week over an eight-week period. Students were asked to bring in assignment drafts or other pieces of writing that they were still working on, and these writing samples were then discussed during the meeting. Because of the individualized nature of the meetings, discussions covered a wide range of topics such as what the writer hoped to communicate through the text, sentence-level concerns about clarity, and analysis of the assigned task. The consultants were directed not to edit or attempt to evaluate the academic quality of the writing, but rather to engage the students in explicit discussion of their writing while verbalizing a reader's perspective.

The following section addresses the program's effectiveness as indicated by a survey administered to the participating students. The next section describes the pre- and post-assessments of student writing, and the conclusion discusses issues that may wish to be addressed in future iterations of the program.

Student Evaluation of Program

At the final meeting of the eight-week program, the students were asked to complete a survey of their attitudes toward writing, working with a writing consultant, and their participation in the program. The following discussion details the results, but in general the survey showed that:

- the students' attitudes toward their writing abilities were significantly more positive at the end of the semester than at the beginning;
- they became significantly more aware of issues related to audience through their participation in the program;
- they had a positive appraisal of their work with the writing consultants; and
- they were positive about their general involvement with the writing program.

Figure 4.4 (continued)

Attitudes toward Writing Ability

Two sets of paired item questions measured the students' attitudes toward their writing abilities at the beginning and end of the semester. For all items, students were asked to show their agreement on a scale of 1 to 5, with higher numbers indicating more positive feelings. As shown in Table 1, the students were significantly more positive in their appraisal of their own writing ability at the end of the semester than at the beginning. The table reports the beginning and end of semester means for each paired item and the respective significance level associated with a paired sample T-test.

Table 1: Attitudes toward Writing Ability

Paired Items*	Beginning Semester Mean	End Semester Mean	Beginning Semester Standard Deviation	End Semester Standard Deviation	Significance
I was/am able to communicate ideas effectively in writing.	3.82	4.05	.89	.64	.03
I was/am able to organize my thoughts well.	3.74	4.09	.92	.59	.00
I always understood / understand what writing assignments were / are asking for.	3.78	4.08	.94	.65	.00
I was/am comfortable with the kind of English used in an academic setting.	4.01	4.19	.85	.62	.05
I was able to / have learned to evaluate my own writing and revise it accordingly.	3.39	3.92	1.17	.63	.00
I felt confident in my writing abilities. / I am confident of my writing ability.	3.51	3.94	1.11	.70	.00

* The beginning of semester items were prefaced by a statement referring to the students' attitudes before the program started (e.g. "before working with a writing consultant," or "at the beginning of this program").

Figure 4.4 (continued)

Awareness of Audience

As reported in Table 2, three pairs of statements measured the students' awareness of audience at the start and end of the program. For each pair, students report a significantly higher awareness of audience at the end of semester as measured by a paired-samples T test.

Table 2: Awareness of Audience

Paired Items*	Beginning Semester Mean	End Semester Mean	Beginning Semester Standard Deviation	End Semester Standard Deviation	Significance
I always thought/think about how my papers would/will sound to someone else.	3.72	4.19	1.12	.68	.00
I could write something that professors would like. / I am able to write papers that professors will appreciate.	3.86	4.08	.92	.71	.03
I was/am open to criticism about my writing.	4.29	4.43	.78	.54	.06

* The beginning of semester items were prefaced by a statement referring to the students' attitudes before the program started (e.g. "before working with a writing consultant," or "at the beginning of this program").

Assessment of Student Writing Abilities

Initial referrals to the writing program were based primarily on a timed writing sample written during the summer orientation in which the students wrote a letter to an editor about the significance of statistics showing increased plagiarism at universities. The papers were holistically evaluated by a team of raters who had been calibrated using benchmark writing samples. Each paper was assessed twice, and the raters, who had all worked as writing consultants in the Writing Center, were asked to decide if the writer could benefit from working with a writing consultant. If they were not sure, they could recommend that a second sample be consulted before a decision was made. In those instances, the Writing Center's Assessment Coordinator examined an opinion essay originally submitted as part of the student's admission application and made a final recommendation. This process identified 100 students who it was felt would benefit from participation.

Figure 4.4 (continued)

At the end of the semester a two-part assessment was conducted to identify students who no longer needed to be required to meet with a consultant. First, the consultant who had been working with the student was asked to recommend whether the student would benefit from continuing, and second, a timed writing sample produced during the last meeting was holistically evaluated. The writing sample was a statement directed toward future XXXX students about what they wish they had known before starting the program. It was rated using a four-point holistic scale that emphasized sophistication of content, organization and rhetorical control, and the use of language. Each paper was rated twice, with the final score being the average of the two ratings. In only two out of 83 instances did the ratings differ by more than one point, and in those cases the Assessment Coordinator assigned the final score. A score of 2.5 on the 4 point scale was considered to be an indication that the student should possibly continue in the program; a 3 or above was considered evidence that a student may be ready to exit.

Table 5 summarizes the end of semester assessment results. Out of 92 students who signed up to work with a consultant, 60 were recommended to exit, 38 to continue during the spring semester, and 2 could not be evaluated because of lack of participation. Fifteen of these recommendations were based solely on the consultant's perspective since the students were either absent from the final meeting or promised to come at a later time to complete the sample and did not. Out of the 83 students who submitted the final writing sample, 12 students requested to continue and so were automatically recommended to do so. Of the remaining 71 cases, the consultant's recommendation and the final writing score were in agreement in 51 cases (72 percent). In the 20 cases where there was a discrepancy, the Assessment Coordinator individually reviewed the consultant's recommendation as well as the beginning and end of the semester writing samples. In 13 of the 20 cases, the Coordinator agreed with the consultant's recommendation, bringing the overall percentage of cases in which the consultant's recommendation was followed to 90 percent (64/71).

Figure 4.4 (continued)

Table 5: Summary of Student Recommendations	
Initially Assessed	**146**
Not referred for participation	*38*
Referred	*100*
Referred but did not participate	*8*
Recommendation to Continue	**38**
Student Request	*12*
Low Writing Sample Rating and Consultant Recommendation	*13*
High Writing Sample but Consultant Recommendation	*3*
Low Writing Sample and Coordinator's Recommendation	*3*
Consultant Recommendation/No Writing Sample	*7*
Recommendation to Exit	**60**
High Writing Sample Rating and Consultant Recommendation	*38*
Low Writing Sample Rating but Consultant Recommendation	*10*
High Writing Sample Rating and Coordinator's Recommendation	*4*
Consultant Recommendation/No Writing Sample	*8*
Unable to Evaluate	**2**

Issues for Future Consideration

Evidence from the student evaluations as well as the assessments of their writing indicates that the program has helped the majority of participating students improve their academic writing abilities. The program's benefits extend beyond this immediate context, however, for it has also served as a catalyst for a number of discussions about the teaching and learning of writing within the XXXX College. Ideas generated in these meetings include:

- identifying writing intensive courses within the curriculum and assigning writing consultants to work with those classes
- broadening the scope of the program to work with all entering students so that the consultants are seen not as agents of remediation but as providers of an outside perspective that is useful for any writer
- the hosting of "brown bag" lunches or workshops for faculty to address topics such as alternatives for assessing writing, cross-cultural perspectives on writing, and the roots of error
- using a workshop series to deliver an actual writing curriculum
- increasing feedback to students concerning the results of the various writing assessments

Source: Written by D. Reynolds for the University of Houston Writing Center

Figure 4.5. Experimental Study (Example Report 5)

Summary Report:
BIOL 3201 Writing Assessment Project

This report summarizes the findings of a comparative study of BIOL 3201 term project papers written before and after the introduction of targeted writing support into the course curriculum. The study was conducted by the UH Writing Center at the request of the College of Natural Sciences and Mathematics. As shown below, papers written subsequent to the curriculum changes were found to exhibit better overall writing quality as well as significantly better abstract, results, and discussion sections.

Project Description

The papers rated for the study were a formal write-up of a genetics laboratory term project in which students applied scientific experimentation and analysis to identify specific mutations in *Drosophila melanogaster* (fruit fly). Guidelines for the papers were provided in the students' laboratory manual and specified that the paper should include abstract, introduction, materials and methods, discussion, and results sections. During the spring and fall semesters of 2005, a rubric specifying writing objectives was introduced, students were given a workshop on writing scientific reports, and course teaching assistants were provided with a workshop on teaching and grading the papers.

This study compared a random sampling of papers written prior to the Spring 2005 semester with a random sampling of papers written in the Fall 2005 semester. Originally 40 papers from each group were selected. One paper from the Fall 2005 semester was subsequently excluded from the study when it was discovered that some of the original pages were missing. Papers from both sampling periods were photocopied and any identifying marks such as names, dates, and grades were blacked out.

Papers were rated by Writing Center staff members, all of whom were working on or had completed graduate degrees and who had some familiarity with scientific writing. The raters were given a rubric developed by the Writing Center in consultation with faculty from the Department of Biology and trained using sample papers for each of the levels in the rubric. The rubric asked raters to assign separate level scores for the abstract, introduction, materials and methods, discussion, and results section as well as for overall writing quality (4=fully and completely meets all objectives . . . 1= serious deficiencies with respect to objectives). Each paper was read by two raters. The final score for each section was the average of the two raters' scores (e.g., Rater 1=3, Rater 2=4, Final Score=3.5). In cases where the raters disagreed by more than one point, the paper was read by a third rater, and the two scores that were in closest agreement were used to compute the average.

Results

Table 1 (page 100) provides mean scores for each of the sections as well as the overall writing quality. As indicated, prior to the curriculum changes the mean score for each area—except materials and methods—was below two (2=addresses some objectives but not all), with the

Figure 4.5 (continued)

Results section producing the lowest mean. Subsequent to instruction the results section showed improvement but was still below two. All other scores were above two, indicating on average at least partial mastery of the objectives for the assignment.

Table 1: Descriptive Statistics

	Sample	Mean	Std. Deviation	N
Abstract	Pre Post	1.96 2.55	.80 .84	40 39
Introduction	Pre Post	1.96 2.21	.82 .78	40 39
Materials and Methods	Pre Post	2.33 2.36	.81 .74	40 39
Results	Pre Post	1.46 1.77	.52 .74	40 39
Discussion	Pre Post	1.74 2.19	.53 .67	40 39
Overall	Pre Post	1.88 2.32	.56 .62	40 39

A multivariate analysis of variance procedure indicated that the effect of the sampling period on the writing scores was significant ($F=3.60$, $p=.004$, $\eta^2 = .231$), suggesting that the changes in the curriculum benefited the students.

Table 2 shows the results of individual analyses of variance run to test the effect on the individual sections. As indicated, the improvement shown in the ratings for the abstracts, results, discussions, and overall writing quality were significant at $p<.05$ or greater.

Table 2: Individual ANOVAs for the effect of the sample period on each score

Dependent Variable	F	Sig.	η^2
Abstract	10.22	.00	.12
Introduction	1.81	.18	.02
Materials and Methods	.04	.85	.00
Results	4.52	.04	.06
Discussion	11.31	.00	.13
Overall	11.13	.00	.13

These findings suggest that the joint efforts of the Writing Center and the Biology Department to target student writing in BIO 3201 during 2005 benefited students in that they are better able to meet the expectations for the term project paper. Analysis of the individual means for Fall 2005, however, indicates that there is room for continued progress in each of the areas, which further collaboration will more than likely facilitate.

Source: Written by D. Reynolds for the University of Houston Writing Center

CHAPTER 5

Worksheets

The worksheets follow.

Program Description

Embeddedness within the Curriculum

Sponsor (Check all that apply):

☐ Provost's Office ☐ College ☐ Department

☐ Course Instructor ☐ Other ________________

Scope of Program:

☐ University-wide ☐ College/Department-wide

☐ Degree-wide ☐ Attached to a course

☐ University-entry ☐ College/Department-entry

☐ Degree-entry ☐ Exit Requirement

Why are the sponsors interested in the program?

Students

Attendance:

☐ Required ☐ Voluntary

Scope:

☐ All students in unit where program is located ☐ Selected students

What is the students' motivation for participating in the program?

Type of Interaction Involved
Presentation of information: ☐ Workshop ☐ Class instruction ☐ Textbooks and/or online materials Interaction based: ☐ Assigned Consultations ☐ Walk-in Consultations ☐ Extensive group work Indirect: ☐ Instructor Training ☐ Materials provided
What kinds of student learning are promoted by the nature of the interaction?

Intensity
Number of Instructional Interactions: ☐ Single ☐ Limited (2–3) ☐ Extended (4+) Time Duration: _____ weeks
What are reasonable expectations for student learning given the intensity of program contact?

Role of Writing for Participants

Frequency in Discipline:

☐ Infrequent ☐ Addressed in specific course(s)

☐ Common Course Requirement

Frequency in Writing Program (if different from discipline):

☐ Single assignment ☐ 2 assignments

☐ Multiple assignments

Discipline's perspective on writing:

☐ Basic communication skill required of college graduate

☐ Critical-thinking tool

☐ Genre mastery necessary for degree

☐ Means for determining course grades

☐ Job requirement

Other:

How are participants in the program likely to conceive of writing?

Working with Example Goal Statements

I. Using this list of program types, indicate the types of programs that might employ the following goal statements. Indicate all that apply.

a) workshops
b) targeted instruction based on a diagnostic assessment
c) programs providing help on a single assignment
d) consultations for all students in a degree program

1. __________ Students will be able to describe differences between clinical and academic writing.

2. __________ Students will be able to produce an appropriate resume for an entry-level position.

3. __________ Students will be able to incorporate and synthesize information from multiple sources in their writing.

4. __________ Students will be able to generate multiple drafts that lead to an improved final product.

5. __________ Students will be able to edit their writing for standard usage.

6. __________ Students will feel confident that they can write for academic courses.

7. __________ Students will be able to explain and justify the organization for a piece of writing.

8. __________ Students will demonstrate an understanding of the audience for a research study proposal.

II. The goal statements in Part I do not specify how we might know if the goal had been achieved (i.e., how to measure it). How might they be measured? The first one has been done for you.

1. by listing three characteristics of clinical writing that do not apply to academic writing

2.

3.

4.

5.

6.

7.

8.

Goals Development

Focus
Content Scope: ☐ Specific Needs ☐ Global Development ☐ Both Directionality: ☐ Redress past ☐ Promote progress ☐ Both
Will goals need to focus on ensuring that certain standards are met, that participants have changed, or both?

Orientation
What do program activities address? ☐ tasks (e.g., producing abstracts) ☐ skills (e.g., organization, mechanics) ☐ content (e.g., APA style, reporting verbs) ☐ processes (e.g., invention, editing) ☐ psychological (e.g., confidence, awareness)
How can the goals reflect the way stakeholders think of the program's activities?

Goals Development 2

Desired Impact
For Individuals 1.____________________ 2.____________________ 3.____________________ For the curriculum 1.____________________ 2.____________________ 3.____________________ For external stakeholders 1.____________________ 2.____________________ 3.____________________

As means for specifying the purpose of the program, use what you have just written to make a list of eight areas that might be appropriate for program goals and specify a desired performance criterion for each. Finally, try to reduce your list to between three and five,

1.____

2.____

3.____

4.____

5.____

6.____

7.____

8.____

Formative Assessments

I. List all assessment tools to be used here (e.g., strategy survey, initial writing sample, focus group, mid-term test).

1.

2.

3.

4.

II. Using the tool numbers, indicate which audiences and formative purposes they will serve in the chart.

	Student	Instructors	Partnering Unit	Writing Center
Diagnostic				
Feedback				
Retrospective				

Summative Assessment

I. For each example goal, check the type of baseline being used for comparison.

Goal	Data	Measure	Baseline for Comparison	Type of Baseline
Students will be able to produce an appropriate résumé for an entry-level position.	Résumé written at end of workshop	Rated as satisfactory or unsatisfactory by two trained raters	Benchmark examples of satisfactory and unsatisfactory résumés generated during pilot study and reviewed by discipline-area faculty.	☐ previous performance ☐ performance of earlier students ☐ external criteria ☐ control group
Students will be able to generate multiple drafts that lead to an improved final product.	Portfolio	Checklist of criteria for improvement (longer, fewer mechanical problems, greater coherence)	Criteria for improved writing drawn from instructor's expertise	☐ previous performance ☐ performance of earlier students ☐ external criteria ☐ control group
Students will feel confident that they can write for academic courses.	Attitudinal survey administered at beginning and end of program	Mean Likert scale response to items related to confidence in writing ability	Statistical significance of difference between class mean at beginning and end of semester	☐ previous performance ☐ performance of earlier students ☐ external criteria ☐ control group
Students will demonstrate an understanding of the audience for a research study proposal.	Grant proposals written by graduate students who attended workshop and ones who did not	Ratings of audience appeal assigned by two trained raters	Scores for students who attended compared with students who did not	☐ previous performance ☐ performance of earlier students ☐ external criteria ☐ control group

II. Setting up your own assessment study
(Check all that apply and then complete the chart.)

Purpose of assessment study

☐ provide descriptive information about students ☐ measure change

Baseline(s) for student performance

☐ previous performance (students compared to themselves)

☐ earlier group of students (e.g., students from previous program or pilot study)

☐ control group

☐ external criteria (e.g., syllabus)

Tools appropriate for generating data needed to measure goals

☐ writing samples ☐ faculty/reader surveys

☐ student attitudinal surveys ☐ observations of performance

Other

Goal	Data	Measure	Baseline for Comparison

Resource Evaluation

Assessment Description (include number of students to be assessed)

Personnel Needs

Roles	Responsible Party	Number of People	Hours per Person
Instrument Design			
Data Elicitation/ Collection (e.g., test supervisor)			
Evaluation of Data (e.g., raters, rater training)			
Data entry/ Clerical support			
Data analysis (e.g., statistical analyst)			

Space Requirements

What space will be needed to conduct assessment or analyze data?

For how long will it be needed?

Time Requirements

How long will it take to design assessment instruments?

How long will it take to collect data?

How long will it take to analyze and report on data?

Writing Assessment Plan

Program Description

Goals

1.

2.

3.

4.

5.

Formative Assessments That Promote Attainment of Goals

Data Tool	Purpose	How Reported

Summative Assessments That Measure Attainment of Goals

Goal	Data Tool	Measure	Baseline Standards for Comparison

Timeline

Data Tool	Collection Date	Reporting Date

Resources Required

(N.B. Complete a copy of this page for each data tool used.)

Data Tool: ______________________________

Personnel

Role	Responsible Parties	Total Number of Hours

Space

Location	Time Needed

Time Required for

Design:

Collection:

Analysis and Reporting:

Observation Record

INSTRUCTOR ____

COURSE ____

Interaction Type: I (Instructor Fronted) / I-C (Instructor—Class interaction) / I-S (Instructor—Student interaction) / S-S (Pair or Group Work) / S (Students working individually)

Time	Interaction Type	Activity Description	General Comments / Suggestions

Observation Evaluation

Focus of Observation	Weak	Adequate	Strong	Comments
Clarity of Lesson Objectives				
Lesson Organization				
Time Management				
Control of Content				
Responsiveness / Adaptability				
Provision of Feedback				
Other:				

Evaluator: ______________________________ Date: ____________________

Reliability Worksheet

Potential Influences on Production of Performance Data	Check if influences production of data	Check if influence needs to be minimized
Student		
• cognitive ability (e.g., task is complex)	☐	☐
• test-taking experience	☐	☐
• familiarity with U.S. academic culture	☐	☐
• demographics (e.g., gender, nationality, age)	☐	☐
• previous academic experience	☐	☐
• psychological state at time of collection	☐	☐
• Other:		☐
Tool		
• time allotted	☐	☐
• place collected	☐	☐
• time collected	☐	☐
• instructions	☐	☐
• content (e.g., prompt topics, reading)	☐	☐
• Other:		☐
Describe what can be done to minimize any unwanted influences on the production of the data.		

Potential Influences on Evaluating Performance Data	Check if influences evaluation of data	Check if influence needs to be minimized
Rater		
• training	☐	☐
• rating experience	☐	☐
• discipline familiarity	☐	☐
• demographics (e.g., gender, nationality, age)	☐	☐
• physical state at time of evaluation (e.g., hunger)	☐	☐
• psychological state at time of collection	☐	☐
• Other:		☐
Tool		
• time allotted for evaluation	☐	☐
• place evaluated	☐	☐
• time evaluated	☐	☐
• ease of recording evaluation	☐	☐
• clarity of tool wording	☐	☐
• Other:		☐

Describe what can be done to minimize any unwanted influences on the evaluation of the data.

Validity Worksheet

Assessment Tool:

What should the tool measure?

Which of the following does your description most resemble:

- ☐ content topic(s) based in a syllabus or course goal statement
- ☐ a general ability that might be measured by other tools as well
- ☐ a theoretical understanding of the ability or abilities
- ☐ desirable consequences of a program
- ☐ what students or stakeholders think is important

How might you collect additional information that would help you verify that the tool is measuring these things?

Glossary

attitudinal survey—instrument used to explore what individuals believe; typically employs series of statements about which respondents indicate the degree to which they agree or disagree; useful for exploring what individuals believe they know how to do as a result of a program of instruction (page 24)

benchmark essays—writing samples used as examples of performance at difference levels; useful for promoting consistency in the application of evaluation criteria across writing samples and between raters (pages 18, 19, 41)

categorical data—type of **discrete data** measured by group membership; examples include belonging to a particular age group, gender, or nationality; distinction is important for choosing statistical procedures that can be used to verify a hypothesis about the data (pages 68, 76)

checklist—type of **evaluation guide** that directs rater to indicate whether a quality or behavior is evidenced or not (page 46)

coding system—guidelines for analyzing **qualitative data** that provide labels for different analytical categories; makes it easier to identify similarities in the data; may be used to impose a **quantitative analysis** on qualitative data by counting instances of particular categories (page 65)

concurrent validity—approach to determining meaningfulness and usefulness of an assessment instrument; focuses on whether the instrument generates results that are similar to those of another instrument that purports to measure the same thing(s) (page 82)

construct validity—approach to determining meaningfulness and usefulness of an assessment instrument; focuses on whether the instrument measures concepts and abilities that are appropriate for it to measure or, in other words, is based on a sound understanding of what it is trying to measure (page 82)

content validity—approach to determining meaningfulness and usefulness of an assessment instrument; focuses on whether the instrument measures the concepts or abilities that it claims to measure (page 82)

continuous data—type of **quantitative data** for which it is reasonable or meaningful to consider portions of a unit; values can be arrayed on number line; examples include counts, such as number of words or percentages; distinction between continuous and **discrete** is important for choosing statistical procedures that can be used to verify a hypothesis about the data (page 76)

control group—in an **experimental study,** the group of subjects that are tested but do not receive any special **treatment;** if you are interested in whether a program of instruction is effective, this would be a group that did not receive the instruction but to whom it would be reasonable to compare the ones who did receive the instruction (page 18)

criterion-referenced—evaluation method in which performance goals or criteria are specified, and performance is evaluated as having achieved (or not) the goal(s) (pages 18, 19)

Cronbach's alpha—statistical measure for the degree to which a group of items on a survey or test generates consistent responses; values range from zero, meaning low consistency, to one, meaning complete consistency; note that consistent does not imply identical; thus responses are consistent if some individuals tend to respond positively to one item and negatively to another, while other individuals respond negatively to the first item and positively to the second (page 56)

descriptive—indicates that the primary purpose of data analysis is to characterize a group of individuals or their performance; examples might be information about the number of participants, an average score, or a statement about a frequently made claim (page 78)

descriptor—prose expression of a **performance level** in an **evaluation guide** (pages 40, 78)

direct evidence—when data closely correspond to what is being measured (such as using a paper to evaluate whether students have learned to write better papers) (page 23)

discrete data—type of **quantitative data** for which it is not reasonable to consider portions of a unit; examples include a characteristic where an individual either belongs or does not belong, such as a nationality, or a performance level where you have to be at one level or the other but cannot be in between; distinction is important for choosing statistical procedures that can be used to verify a hypothesis about the data (page 76)

elicited evidence—data generated in response to an instrument created specifically for the purpose of evaluating a hypothesis; an example would be using a questionnaire about the helpfulness of a tutorial to evaluate the effectiveness of visits to a writing center (page 23)

evaluation guide—systematic procedure such as a rubric or coding sheet that determines how evidence will be interpreted for the purposes of making conclusions (page 23)

experimental study—method for evaluating a hypothesis (such as, students can write better paragraphs because of the workshops they attended) in which the participants are randomly divided into one or more groups that receive a **treatment** (examples might be attending a 2-session workshop and attending a 4-session workshop) and a **control group** that receives no treatment (in other words, they did not attend any workshop) (pages 18, 19)

face validity—approach to determining meaningfulness and usefulness of an assessment instrument; focuses on whether the way in which the instrument is designed makes sense to the respondents given its stated purpose(s) (page 82)

focus group—procedure for eliciting commonly held beliefs by asking groups of individuals to discuss a topic or respond to questions; data are typically analyzed for recurring themes and similarity of responses across groups (pages 24, 65, 76)

formative assessment—evaluation that generates information that can be used to improve current performance; often seen as a tool for learning because of its immediate applicability; an example might be an instructor's comments on the draft of a paper (page 5)

holistic rubric—**evaluation guide** that directs rater to consider overall effect or quality of the writing or other product being evaluated; may identify qualities that contribute to effect or quality but does not weigh them individually; typically specifies descriptions for different **performance levels** (page 39)

indirect evidence—when data provide an indication of what is being measured or information on which inferences can be based; necessary if what is being measured cannot be observed; example would be using responses to questionnaire about how an essay was planned to understand planning process (page 23)

inferential—indicates that the primary purpose of data analysis is to determine if a relationship exists; examples include information that suggests students perform better after a course of instruction or that non-native speakers tend to interpret a test question in a certain way (page 78)

institutional effectiveness—method for evaluating academic and administrative units relative to performance goals or outcomes as opposed to, for example, amount spent on projects or infrastructure; method currently promoted by many accrediting bodies (page 4)

interval data—type of **continuous data** where the magnitude of the difference between two values can be measured and can be compared to the magnitude of the difference between two other variables; differs from **ordinal data** where it is not possible to determine how much greater a higher value is than a lesser, only that it is higher; examples include measures of time or length; distinction is important for choosing statistical procedures that can be used to verify a hypothesis about the data (page 76)

items—individual questions or statements on a survey (page 55)

Likert-like scale—common system for measuring responses on a survey; provides respondents with a continuum of verbal characterizations of agreement to choose from, such as strongly agree/agree/no opinion/disagree/strongly disagree; levels on the continuum are then converted to numerical representations to allow for **quantitative** analysis of the data (page 56)

longitudinal study—method for investigating a research question that depends on collecting multiple pieces of data produced over time by each participant; often focuses on understanding how individuals develop knowledge or skills (page 19)

mean—the average of a group of numbers; calculated by adding the numbers together and then dividing by how many numbers you have; one way of representing the center value of a group of numbers (page 74)

measurement—system for informing judgments about data; often thought of as procedures for quantifying data but may also refer to a qualitative taxonomy used to code data (pages 10, 20, 82)

median—when a group of numbers are arranged from low to high, it is the middle value of the set; if there are an odd number of terms in the group (e.g., 45, 45, 52, 63, 71), then it is the value that has an equal number of terms with higher and lower values (i.e., 52); if the number of terms is even (e.g., 45, 52, 63, 71), then it is the **mean** of the two middle values (i.e., 52+63/2 = 57.5) (pages 77, 78)

natural evidence—data originally produced for reasons other than evaluating a hypothesis; example would be using a paper from a history course assignment to evaluate effectiveness of visits to writing center (page 23)

norming population—group of individuals whose performance on a task or test is used as a baseline for comparisons; when evaluating the performance of subsequent groups it is important to understand ways in which differences between the two groups or their experiences might explain differences in their performance (page 18)

norm-referenced test—assessment instrument where achievement is measured relative to the performance of a **norming population;** also referred to as a **standardized test** (pages 18, 19)

objective test—test for which respondents' answers can be marked as correct, incorrect, or possibly partially correct as opposed to qualitatively better or worse; common question types include fill-in-the-blank, matching, and multiple choice; typically used to measure retention of factual knowledge (page 28)

ordinal data—type of **discrete data** where values indicate ranking or ordering; examples include essay ratings and indications of agreement; distinction is important for choosing statistical procedures that can be used to verify a hypothesis about the data (page 76)

percentile ranks—method for measuring performance; process begins by ranking individuals in a **norming** population based on their performance and then dividing them into equal–sized groups (such as lowest 10 percent, second 10 percent, third 10 percent, etc.); range of actual scores for each group (such as lowest 10 percent got fewer than 30 questions correct, next 10 percent got 30–36 correct answers) are then used to set standard for evaluating future groups assessed with same instrument; results for subsequent groups are reported according to the percentile group they fall into rather than the number of correct answers (page 19)

performance levels—set of constructs created by an **evaluation guide** for describing demonstrated knowledge or ability; allows a rater to rank whatever is being evaluated relative to independent criteria (page 40)

pilot—small-scale study conducted as a precursor to a larger study with the purpose of refining or validating study methodology; may also be used to justify the need for a large-scale study (pages 28, 60, 68)

placement tests—assessments used to determine which course a student should take (pages 4, 19)

positivistic—characterized by a belief that knowledge should be based on experience as opposed to, for example, reasoning about hypothetical situations; commonly associated with the scientific method and the use of an experimental approach to verify a claim or conclusion (page 74)

pre/post study—method for evaluating change as the result of an experience such as a program of instruction in which the same or similar instruments are used to evaluate an individual's knowledge before and after the experience (pages 17, 19, 43)

predictive validity—approach to determining meaningfulness and usefulness of an assessment instrument; focuses on whether the results are confirmed by subsequent performance (page 82)

prompt—question, assignment, or set of instructions used to initiate and direct the production of data; example would be an essay question (page 25)

protocol—systematic procedure for collecting data such as a guide for taking notes during an observation of a class or list of questions to ask during an interview (page 45)

qualitative data—data that are not represented **quantitatively** and that are analyzed through a process of reasoned inferences about common themes, similarities and differences, distinctive responses; common examples include narrative responses to questions, **transcripts,** or observation notes (pages 65, 73, 75)

quantitative—approach to characterizing data in terms of numerical symbols; allows for judgments about data to be derived from mathematical analysis (pages 48, 75)

quantitative data—data that are represented numerically and analyzed in terms of mathematical relations; examples include scores on a test, percentages, rankings of performance (pages 48, 75, 80)

quasi-experimental study—method for evaluating a hypothesis (such as, students can write better paragraphs because of the workshops they attended) in which participants are divided into one or more groups that receive a **treatment** (examples might be attending a 2-session workshop and attending a 4-session workshop) and a group that received no treatment (in other words, they did not attend any workshop); more common in educational settings than **experimental studies** because does not require that participants be randomly assigned to the different groups, making it possible to use existing-intact classes (pages 18, 19, 44)

questionnaire—data elicitation tool where questions are used to prompt student reflection on learning (pages 7, 24, 51, 69, 76)

ratio data—type of **continuous data** where scale is created by measuring one type of **interval data** relative to another; examples include number of clauses per sentence in a text or the average score on a test; distinction is important for choosing statistical procedures that can be used to verify a hypothesis about the data (page 76)

record—term used to describe set of data in a database belonging to a particular case; often corresponds to an individual (page 67)

reliability analysis—procedure for evaluating usefulness of a piece of data such as the answers of a group of students to a question on a test or survey; evaluation is based on whether the data is consistent with other data that we think it should be consistent with, such as a similar question or the same question asked to a similar group of students (pages 56, 80)

rubric—guide for evaluating data; typically specifies traits that will be evaluated and criteria for determining performance (pages 18, 27, 39)

scale—term applied to a group of **items** on a survey that are assumed to measure the same attitude or belief; validity of this assumption may be measured by a **reliability analysis** (page 56)

significance values—measures of whether or not the acceptance of a hypothesis is **statistically significant** (page 74)

standardized test—assessment instrument where achievement is measured relative to the performance of a **norming population**; also referred to as a **norm-referenced test** (pages 18, 19)

statistical significance—when statistical procedures are used to evaluate the likelihood that a claim or hypothesis is valid, this refers to whether a pre-determined criteria for accepting the hypothesis has been met; often signaled by a symbol such as $p < .05$ or $p = .032$, which quantifies the chance that the judgment made (such as, students performed better after instruction than before) was false (in other words, it was just chance that the scores were higher) (page 19)

summative assessment—evaluation that focuses on achievements; end-of-course grade would be an example (pages 5, 43, 46)

survey—instrument that asks respondents to indicate a level of agreement with a belief or opinion (page 55)

systemic validity—approach to determining meaningfulness and usefulness of an assessment instrument; focuses on whether the instrument serves the purposes it claims to serve within the context of the learning environment (page 82)

trait rubric—**evaluation guide** that directs rater to consider one or more specific aspects of the writing or other product being evaluated, such as content, organization, and language usage; often provides descriptions of **performance levels** for each aspect;

may also specify system for combining judgments about different aspects into an overall judgment of the product, such as weighting each aspect equally and then summing the scores (page 39)

transcripts—written representation of an oral conversation; should employ systematic procedures for representing characteristics of oral interaction such as speaker identity, pauses in speech, multiple individuals speaking at the same time, changes in speaker tone for the purpose of signaling emotion, and segmentation of informational content (page 29)

treatment—in the context of an **experimental** or **quasi-experimental study**, the instruction or other intervention whose effectiveness is being evaluated (page 18)

turn—linguistic term for unit of speech produced by an individual in a conversation; boundaries typically marked by a change of speaker; everything the individual says until the next speaker begins talking (page 35)

validity—degree to which an instrument measures what it is suppose to measure (page 82)

variable—term in a mathematical equation or relationship that could have multiple values (page 78)